John Franklin

Status

4 August 86

Foreword

Clinical psychology is a rapidly expanding area of inquiry and practice. Traditional lines between clinical and other sub-disciplines of psychology are rapidly eroding. Research in information processing has direct impact on behavior therapy, work in physiological psychology affects our work in biofeedback, community psychologists need to keep abreast of what is happening in social psychology, and so on. At the same time, clinical psychologists are being called on to work in a variety of new settings, and to continually develop new skills as well as utilize their existing skills. Health Maintenance organizations (HMOs) ask clinical psychologists not only to provide direct clinical service to clients but also to help change the health-related behaviors of clients who do not require

73227

direct service. Community mental health centers ask their clinicians to provide direct service, and to assist in developing prevention programs and program evaluation procedures. These are but a few examples of how the field of clinical psychology is expanding.

It is difficult for the professional practitioner as well as the student of clinical psychology to keep in touch with what is happening in the field. Traditional textbooks can give only superficial coverage to these recent changes and the journal literature does not provide a broad overview. The Addison-Wesley Series in Clinical and Professional Psychology is an effort to fill this gap. Taken as a whole, the series could be used as an introduction to the field of clinical psychology. A subset of these books, such as those on therapy, for example, could serve as a text for a course in therapy. Single volumes can be used for seminars when supplemented by journal articles, or as supplemental texts for courses in which the instructor feels the text is lacking in coverage of that area, or for short courses for the active professional. We hope that each of these volumes, written or edited by experts in the area, will also serve as an up-to-date overview of that area for the interested professional who feels in need of updating.

In this volume, George D. Goldman and Donald S. Milman have brought together a number of contributors to provide an up-to-date perspective on the most traditional of all approaches to psychotherapy-psychoanalysis. The chapters skillfully interweave important conceptual ideas like resistance and transference with the flow of psychoanalytic therapy over time. The reader is thus provided with a real understanding of contemporary psychoanalysis and its many variations.

Webster defines a *primer* as "a small introductory volume on a subject." Goldman and Milman, and their collaborators, have provided exactly such a volume on psychoanalytic psychotherapy.

LEONARD D. GOODSTEIN

Preface

We began this book because we felt a need among upper undergraduate, graduate, and beginning therapists in many areas for a beginning textbook on psychotherapy. It grew out of our many years of direct experience in teaching and developed from our attempts to answer our students' needs for guidance and clarity as they began the complicated process of learning about therapy. Most of the material that has been written in the past is of a very complicated theoretical nature, mainly because it is directed at advanced professionals who have complicated problems of individual cases in their practice that they would like to understand. The very simple everyday aspects of both theory and practice are not readily available in any condensed, understandable form for the beginning therapist. This book attempts to fill that particular gap.

With this goal in mind, we felt that it would be desirable to make the complex metapsychological descriptions of therapy more understandable. We also felt that the complicated cases presented in the literature as examples of psychoanalytic psychotherapy are overly abstract, and we therefore asked our collaborators in each instance to try and provide an understanding of theoretical concepts germane to the practice of psychotherapy, and to proceed from these definitions to concrete examples taken directly from their practice. We have, in all instances, tried to make the theory understandable to a beginning student. We have not tried to oversimplify a very complicated and rigorous procedure, but have tried to avoid making things sound difficult and abstract when simple, direct explanations are possible.

Because the book is directed primarily to a practical and everyday perception of psychotherapy, however, we feel that a proper background to prepare for a metapsychological overview of psychoanalysis and psychoanalytic psychotherapy is in order. In some respects, the material that follows is very broad and highly philosophical. In other respects, it condenses and repeats content that will occur in a more elaborated fashion throughout the book. To many of our readers, this part of the introduction may seem to be too theoretical and too philosophical at this juncture, but we remind them that some of the theoretical discussion will be amplified by further reading in this book, and we suggest that they read through this section a second time after having read the text itself.

Psychoanalysis was evolved and developed by Sigmund Freud. However, people frequently confuse the term psychoanalysis when used to describe the technique of treating patients with the same term used to describe the theory of personality. For most people, the two seem interchangeable and interrelated. However, psychoanalytic theory is a conceptual frame of reference about how human beings function psychologically; whereas psychoanalytic therapy is directed at helping humans understand how to change people's disabled functioning. We will examine first the fundamental concepts of psychoanalysis the therapy, because we feel that an understanding of that aspect of Freudian theory is most germane to understanding this book.

As Freud originally conceptualized psychoanalysis, the major distinguishing feature was the utilization of the concepts of transference and resistance.* The specifics of how this was accomplished are the essence of the technique of psychoanalysis. For Freud and his followers, for many years, any deviation from these basic constructs made the therapeutic technique nonpsychoanalytic. However, in 1958, Eisler, in his very thorough discussion of the metapsychology of psychoanalysis, suggested that "parameters" of the technique were allowed and sometimes necessary in the treatment of different types of disorders. He felt that the major tool in the psychoanalytic process was interpretation. His admonition, however, was that this variation from orthodox technique, this parameter, must be discarded when no longer necessary and orthodox technique resumed.

A further metapsychological construct related to the relationship between the analyst and the patient is the notion of analytic neutrality. This term, employed by Kernberg and others, does not imply an emotional neutrality but is a technical stance wherein the analyst functions equidistantly between the three structures of the mind—the id, superego, and ego. The implicit goal of psychoanalysis is the restructuring of the personality. This was thought best accomplished by a thorough working through, so that patients could understand all of the aspects of their transference neurosis, as well as by the full exploration of all of their resistance to treatment.

In contrast, psychoanalytic psychotherapy is the name given to those therapeutic techniques that utilize the basic concepts of psychoanalysis and, in addition, consistently use the parameters that Eisler had suggested as useful to introduce and then discard. In psychoanalytic therapy, these parameters, then, are maintained throughout the treatment. The goals of psychoanalytic psychotherapy, which are much more limited than the goal of psychoanalysis, are directed toward symptom alleviation and psychological structure changes in certain limited sectors of the individual. The utilization of psychoanalytic psychotherapy has been necessary for a variety of reasons: some patients are not suitable for psychoanalysis; some do not desire a restructuring of their entire personality; and some are either unwilling or unable to expend the time, energy, and money necessary for such a process.

---

*The technical terms that are introduced in this discussion will not be defined or further elaborated at this point, since they are thoroughly discussed in the text itself.

A relevant issue today is the utilization of psychoanalytic psychotherapy in current psychotherapeutic practice. Freud originally cate-
gorized a major group of patients as untreatable by the psychoanalytic method. These patients, who were then broadly cate-
gorized as the narcissistic neurosis and who today would be considered schizoid, borderline, narcissistic, or psychotic, were thought
by Freud to be incapable of developing and working with the usual
object transference and therefore untreatable. In other words, they
were incapable of distinguishing between self and object representations in the therapy. They developed, in psychoanalysis, a
narcissistic transference that at times made them unable to distinguish themselves from the therapists, and also made them unable
to distinguish the therapists from representative human beings from
the past.

In recent years, there has been an extensive exploration of possible methods of treating this large diagnostic group of patients.
The theoretical and technical input in this area has been enormous.
With this group of patients, parameters of treatment had to be
introduced in order for them to be successfully treated. The treatment of these patients utilizes psychoanalytic psychotherapy. The
major focus of all of these approaches has been to move these patients from a narcissistic transference position to an object transference position, but there have been many and varied theories on
how to achieve this goal. It is conceptualized that once a patient
has moved far enough along to develop the usual transference, a
more orthodox psychoanalytic treatment would be feasible. But it is
difficult to be sure that parameters introduced for such an extended
period of time in their treatment can ever be completely worked
through and discarded.

Concomitant with this major shift in treatment techniques over
the past decade has occurred a reorganization and reintegration of
different psychoanalytic theories of personality. In the United
States, the major schools of psychoanalytic thinking have been the
interpersonal ones evolved from Sullivan, Horney, and Fromm, as
well as the more orthodox Freudian position. In England, the two
major schools have been those of Freud and Klein. With the
emphasis on ego psychology over the past twenty-five years, the
Freudian theoretical model is no longer the id-dominated one so
prevalent in the early 1900s. With the introduction of the concepts
of object relatedness, individuation and separation, self-develop-

ment and internal object representation, there has evolved a rapprochement among the various analytic schools. More recently, a representative therapist from any of these schools would have many more areas of common theoretical agreement, although there would still be major areas where they may disagree.

Thus, we see in the changing tide of both psychoanalytic theory and psychotherapeutic technique, varieties of movement that make for modification and innovation and yet congruence. The shifts in both theory and techniques within some of the major theoretical schools have made the description of psychoanalytically oriented psychotherapy presented in this book something psychoanalysts could both integrate and accept.

October 1977   G.D.G.
Garden City, New York   D.S.M.

Contributors

Judith Caligor, Ph.D.; Faculty and Supervisor, Group Therapy Department, Postgraduate Center for Mental Health, New York City; Clinical Associate, Graduate Faculty, New School for Social Research; Private practice.

Leopold Caligor, Ph.D.; Clinical Professor of Psychology and Supervisor of Psychotherapy, Postdoctoral Program in Psychotherapy, Institute of Advanced Psychological Studies, Adelphi University; Faculty, Supervising and Training Analyst, William Alanson White Institute of Psychiatry, Psychoanalysis and Psychology; Private practice.

Marvin Daniels, Ph.D.; Associate Clinical Professor of Psychology and Supervisor of Psychotherapy, Postdoctoral Program in Psychotherapy, Institute of Advanced Psychological Studies, Adelphi University; Member and Faculty, New York Center for Psychoanalytic Training; Associate Member, N.P.A.P.

Ruth-Jean Eisenbud, Ph.D.; Clinical Professor of Psychology and Supervisor of Psychotherapy, Postdoctoral Program in Psychotherapy, Institute of Advanced Psychological Studies, Adelphi University, Associate Professor of Psychotherapy and Psychoanalysis, Postdoctoral Program, New York University; Faculty, N.P.A.P.

George D. Goldman, Ph.D.; Clinical Professor of Psychology, Supervisor of Psychotherapy and Director, Postdoctoral Psychotherapy Center, Institute of Advanced Psychological Studies, Adelphi University; Private practice.

Milton Gurvitz, Ph.D.; Clinical Professor of Psychology and Supervisor of Psychotherapy, Postdoctoral Program in Psychotherapy, Institute of Advanced Psychological Studies, Adelphi University; Director, Great Neck

Consultation Center; Senior Member, National Psychological Association for Psychoanalysis.

Donald S. Milman, Ph.D.; Professor of Psychology and Co-Director, Post-doctoral Program in Psychotherapy, Institute of Advanced Psychological Studies, Adelphi University; Private practice.

Dale H. Ortmeyer, Ph.D.; Clinical Professor of Psychology and Supervisor of Psychotherapy, Postdoctoral Program in Psychotherapy, Institute of Advanced Psychological Studies, Adelphi University; Director, Continuing Professional Education, Fellow and Training Analyst, William Alanson White Institute of Psychiatry, Psychoanalysis and Psychology; Faculty, Westchester Center for the Study of Psychoanalysis and Psychotherapy.

Lorelle Saretsky, Ph.D.; Assistant Director, Postdoctoral Psychotherapy Center, Assistant Clinical Professor, Senior Supervising Psychologist, Institute of Advanced Psychological Studies, Adelphi University; Private practice.

Theodore Saretsky, Ph.D.; Clinical Professor of Psychology and Super-visor of Psychotherapy, Postdoctoral Program in Psychotherapy, Institute of Advanced Psychological Studies, Adelphi University; Private practice.

George Stricker, Ph.D.; Professor of Psychology and Assistant Dean, Institute of Advanced Psychological Studies, Adelphi University; Con-sulting Psychologist, Queens-Nassau Mental Health Service of H.I.P.; Private practice.

Acknowledgments

First we would like to thank our students for their comments and questions on issues they have raised over the years. It is in response to their need that we have written this book. In addition, we are extremely grateful to our secretaries, Marge Burgard, Bernadette Clark, and Terry Mason, for their assistance, support, and dedication throughout this project. They have worked long and hard, and with as much involvement as we could possibly ask of ourselves.

We also thank the various colleagues and friends who have contributed chapters for their patience and flexibility when faced with our many demands, and for their willing cooperation in our joint effort to achieve the high standard of quality we had envisioned. More specifically, we thank George Stricker for coming through like the professional he is always, and giving us his excellent chapter on such short notice.

We are also grateful to Marvin Daniels, not only for his fine chapter but also for his editorial assistance, critical comments, and supportive friendship.

Last but by no means least, we thank our wives, Belle Goldman and Marilyn Milman, for their understanding and patience with us when we spent those many long evenings working on this book.

Contents

Countertransference

The Middle Phase of Treatment

The Dream in Psychoanalytic Therapy

Therapeutic Crises

End Phase of Treatment

Milton S. Gurvitz

An Historical Perspective

There is a popular stereotype nourished by Hollywood and television that in psychoanalytic psychotherapy the patients talk and the charismatic analysts listen. The analysts have a brilliant, intuitive insight. The patients now know their hidden secrets and react dramatically, express great emotion, and are swiftly cured.

Another, more bitter misconception is that patients talk endlessly to bland, minimally responsive, and unseen therapists. Sometime in the distant future they gradually talk themselves out and develop strange feelings for their analysts that reveal their unconscious problems. The analysts summarize in a few pithy sentences and the therapy is successful. If this doesn't happen, it is the *patients* who are *resistant* and cannot be helped. With some resistant patients the process goes on interminably; sometimes with a series of therapists.

There are professional stereotypes, too. Some critics charge that psychoanalytic psychotherapists simply sell conversation and friendship by the hour to lonely, friendless neurotics.

Some *modern* critics say that psychoanalytic psychotherapy has not improved since Freud and is ill adapted to contemporary life. Others say that it is a pessimistic philosophy oriented only to reconciling people to their "discontents" or to the prevailing social order. Naive critics still believe that psychoanalytic psychotherapy is obsessed with sex, preaching not only sexual freedom but liberation from all restraints, and that as a result people are "taught" to think only about themselves and their own selfish needs.

There are also perceptive critics who have pointed out that psychoanalytic psychotherapy, at least as practiced in the past, has been too concerned with inner drives and mechanisms and not enough with people and their interactions.

Psychoanalytic psychotherapy suffers from some of its more extreme advocates. Strangest are those cultists who wish to link psychoanalytic psychotherapy exclusively with medicine. Although very few medical psychoanalytic therapists would feel competent to physically examine their patients, their argument is that somehow it is better if a physician-psychiatrist does it. Certainly it tends to be more expensive.

Other "orthodox analysts" feel that psychoanalytic psychotherapy is not really effective unless it takes place five times a week on a couch. Still others feel that nothing really new has been discovered since Freud. The most extreme feel that psychoanalytic psychotherapy is the answer to *all* human misery and that the ills of the world could be cured by a judicious application of psychoanalytic psychotherapy to everyone; and certainly to anyone who has problems.

What then is psychoanalytic psychotherapy? First of all, it is not a creed handed down by Freud never to be changed. It is a dynamic, growing, developing method of helping people solve psychological problems. In recent years it is being extended and modified to treat human problems that have been beyond help in the past. As we shall see, Freud was the great innovator, but Anna Freud, Erik Erikson, Ralph Greenson, Rene Spitz, Heinz Hartmann and collaborators, Heinz Kohut, and Otto Kernberg are contemporaries making significant contributions. Psychoanalytic psychotherapy is an optimistic, dynamic approach to human problems because it is based on the fundamental proposition that the human ego is ordinarily capable of dealing with life to produce an effective and happy individual. Psychoanalytic psychotherapy, then, is the search for ways to allow the ego to resume its growth potential when it has been interrupted in the life cycle.

The fundamental ideas and approach of psychoanalytic psychotherapy come from the pioneering ideas and clinical investigations of Sigmund Freud. To a remarkable degree he met the problems of all psychotherapists and provided scientific breakthroughs and hypotheses sufficient to rank him with Darwin, Marx, and Einstein as one of the great architects of contemporary society.

When a patient comes to a psychotherapist for help, the nature of the neurotic, intrapsychic conflict soon becomes apparent to the therapist, sometimes even in the first interview. The therapist also knows that it will not help the patient to simply tell him his unconscious conflicts and wishes. The present adjustment, painful as it must be, is the best that this person is capable of at the moment. Even though he comes for help, he will be resistant to any self-knowledge that will subject him to even greater anxiety and pain.

Furthermore, the psychotherapist knows that it is impossible to change the past; if the neurotic conflict is to be resolved it must be taken out of the realm of past history and brought into present reality, the here and now. In short, we have to deal with the patient's resistance both to change and to reversing the regression to earlier forms of adaptation. The work of the therapist, then, is to analyze the resistance of the patient. To do this we are able to use the patient's behavior because it is a compromise between his forbidden wishes and his defenses and resistances to them. We encourage the patient to free associate and communicate whatever comes to mind because this relaxation of the *conscious* control encourages regression in the service of the ego rather than in the service of the resistance. Similarly, we use symptoms, slips of the tongue, and dreams to get at the meaning of resistance. While this interpretation of the resistance will be covered at greater length in this and other chapters, we must emphasize that we have to expect resistance and that when, after having cooperated, the patient appears most resistant, he is telling us what is most crucial in his conflict. Interpretation of resistance always begins with the everyday, surface problems. It is designed to demonstrate to the patient why he is afraid rather than what he is afraid of.

Since the patient does not really want to change his behavior, he looks to the therapist to help him find some way of gratifying his neurotic desires without pain and anxiety. It is the task of the therapist not to be maneuvered into providing this gratification in reality or in fantasy. This forces the patient into the real world.

The patient does require support in initially bearing the pain of dealing with his resistance. The patient needs this support precisely because he has suffered from an inadequate relationship in the past with a significant parental figure. These needs are met by contacting the non-neurotic, healthy aspects of the patient's ego and establishing a therapeutic alliance. Obviously, if this contact is to be therapeutic, the therapist's ego must also be a healthy one. To establish a therapeutic alliance, therapists must be willing to invest their time and energy in the patient. They must have personal qualities of empathy and understanding, and must be nonjudgmental. The patient develops a feeling of support, strength, integrity, and self-esteem sufficient to temporarily make up for his own lack of ego strength. A feeling of basic trust develops when the patient feels that the psychoanalyst lends this strength in the expectation that the patient will grow, and not to make him dependent. This implies a high level of training and security on the part of the therapist. This is not easily achieved, and the patient will initially test the sincerity of the therapist's intentions, both overtly and covertly. Once the therapeutic alliance is started, the patient can begin building his own ego and confronting his resistances. In successful psychoanalytic psychotherapy, the therapeutic alliance becomes detached from the analysis and the analyst and thus becomes part of the ego and the ego ideal.

As the patient settles into a relationship he begins to have nonrational emotions, ideas, and fantasies about the analyst. These represent the unconscious parts of the ego and are a reservoir of feelings and conflicts from childhood and infancy. It is as if the analyst were a lightning rod discharging the pent-up transference feelings that have been repressed into the unconscious.

Instead of remembering the past, the patient unconsciously repeats, as a resistance, these significant events in the transference, thus bringing the past into the analytic hour and allowing the analyst to interpret the transference. The ego is then aided to remember instead of repeat and to grow and achieve insight. Positive transferences center around conflicts over sexuality and loving. Negative transferences range from aggression and dislike to envy and contempt. Most transferences are ambivalent, with the surface transference reaction having its unconscious opposite counterpart.

In analyzing the transference, the patient utilizes his ability to split his ego, aided by the therapeutic alliance. The regressive, irrational, unconscious ego can be revealed in transference. The analyst's intervention brings the patient's objective ego into play, allowing the patient insight into his affect and allowing further growth of the ego.

By releasing resistance, analyzing increases insight through ego growth. It is a process of interpretation that is possible only with symptoms that are felt to be consciously irritating or unwelcome. Such symptoms are called ego-alien. The ego wishes to either expel or assimilate the alien. Symptoms that do not consciously disturb the patient (egosyntonic) have to be postponed until the ego has grown sufficiently that it no longer tolerates the regressive behavior. The growth of the working alliance allows more deeply buried egosyntonic symptoms to be converted to ego-alien resistances, the prerequisite for interpretation. The deepest, most significant ego-alien conflicts are revealed by the strongest transference.

Before we can use the insight and ego-building analytic techniques, it is often necessary to use more supportive, nonanalytic techniques. Abreaction, for example, allows for the release of repressed emotion. By releasing some tension, the patient is able to deal with the remainder in a more insightful way. The emotional intensity makes real the repressed experience and gives a sense of relief. This relief is in itself a resistance unless in turn analyzed to reveal the basic conflict.

The use of suggestion recognizes the infantile, regressive position of the patient. The therapist assumes a parental role and induces helpful ideas and behavior. The patient experiences an unwarranted feeling of confidence and optimism, which helps him face the initial pain of confronting resistance or bringing up unconscious material. If the suggestion is not analyzed, dependence on the analyst persists; if analyzed, the insight into the resistance that made suggestion necessary leads to further ego growth and independence.

Manipulation, although in current disfavor, is a legitimate technique as long as one does *not* assume a deliberate pose. It *is* legitimate to be passive and allow an incipient negative transference to develop into a rage and thus be more easily demonstrated. It is also legitimate to be active and remind the patient of an irritation he is ignoring.

The analyst seeks to determine the unconscious conflicts and resistances of the patient and to gain insight into how the patient got that way and how he now feels. This then must be conveyed to the patient with such timing that the resistances can be overcome and insight and ego growth achieved.

The analyst observes best from a neutral, nondirectional, free-floating position. She allows her senses (even olfactory) to bring her data, which she mixes with her own feelings, empathy, intuition, and introspection. She processes this raw mix with her own observing ego, utilizing critical thinking and theoretical knowledge.

Obviously, the therapist's own needs must be excluded to achieve objectivity. The analyst follows the thread of the patient's productions and behavior until she becomes aware of resistance. If the patient does not recognize the resistance, the therapist at the appropriate time confronts the resistance and makes it meaningful. Once the resistance enters the here and now it can be clarified by bringing into sharp focus the painful feelings or forbidden impulses that are its motives. This, in turn, leads to interpreting the underlying affects, impulses, fantasies, and memories. Sometimes the way or mode of resisting gives us the best clue to the nature of the resistance, especially since it is expressed as part of the transference behavior of the patient. Thus it represents the way in which the infantile conflict was handled in response to primary, interpersonal figures.

In most cases the above process will have to be repeated many times to demonstrate its validity and because resistances tend to repeat. The growing ego accustoms itself to carrying out the process with decreasing help from the analyst. Real insight is achieved only when the mature ego is able to do the bulk of the analytic work itself. Obviously, this takes hours of collaborative effort.

Once the technical aspects of analytic psychotherapy are mastered, the greatest stumbling block for the therapist is her own emotional problems, which lead to her missing or misinterpreting the productions of her patients. The therapist has to be as unsparingly objective and suspicious of her own behavior as she is of her client's. When resistance is encountered, it can be just as much due to the therapist's emotional and unconscious response as to the patient's. The therapist's own unconscious feelings engender anxiety when, instead of operating as a signal, they stir defensive reactions. In one way or another, countertransference leads to hostility toward the patient. The problem becomes even more complicated if the therapist defends herself against the awareness of her hostility by becoming irrationally helpful and overcaring.

The signs of an unresolved countertransference are similar to those of a neurosis: anxiety, excessive fatigue, boredom, and even drowsiness. If the therapist feels that she is *acting* exploitively or angrily or if she would be ashamed if her spouse or colleagues know of her behavior, then she should be wary of her own countertransference reactions.

Countertransference per se is not bad. If analyzed, countertransference can lead to the most profound understandings of the deepest layers of the patient's personality that the therapist is responding to. Just as the patient struggles with his resistance, the therapist struggles between her desires to understand the patient and her own resistance to the pain and anxiety of sharing and feeling the patient's problems that reactivate her own human failings. In mastering the countertransference, the therapist not only helps her patient but achieves her own ego growth. This process underlines the collaborative nature of psychoanalytic psychotherapy. Furthermore, it illuminates the necessity for the psychoanalytic psychotherapist to be thoroughly analyzed as the *beginning* of a professional lifetime of self-analysis.

Contemporary psychoanalytic psychotherapy has direct and major roots in the work of its founder, Sigmund Freud. Freud began his medical career in 1886 at age thirty, treating primarily hysterical women. Despite the prevailing opinion that the cause of hysteria was organic, Freud found that under hypnosis, suggestion alone helped to alleviate hysterical symptoms. From Breuer, an older colleague, Freud learned that in the patient, Anna O., symptoms disappeared under hypnosis when she recalled with great emotion the traumatic sexual events that were too painful for her to remember. So shocking was this, at the height of Victorian prudery, that Breuer did not care to try hypnosis again, but Freud bravely persisted and found it significantly helpful. He came to the then startling conclusion that the neuroses were psychological in etiology and that remembering the trauma and releasing the unexpressed emotion had a therapeutic effect. So revolutionary was the whole subject that only with great reluctance did Breuer consent to publish their joint results in 1895 (Breuer and Freud 1895; Jones 1953).

Dissatisfied with hypnosis because some patients could not be hypnotized, Freud found he could get better results by pressing the woman's head as she lay on the couch and strongly suggesting that she could and would remember, assisting her by being alert to cues and hints. Finally, at the suggestion of Frau Von R. that she be allowed to simply talk, Freud discovered free association, the spontaneous talking of the patient without conscious censoring until resistance is overcome (Jones 1953).

As are *all* potential therapists, Freud was psychologically ill equipped to deal with the impact of his patients' problems and revelations on his own emotional stability. At a time when sex was taboo and the sight of a lady's ankle was sexually suggestive, Freud was being deluged with erotic and aggressive "revelations." Far from being elated, Freud complained of difficulty in working and, on the death of his father in 1896, became depressed, phobic, and fearful of dying of heart symptoms (Jones 1953). Characteristically, instead of fleeing, Freud plunged into a four-year period of self-analysis, during which he found that dreams have symbolic meaning and can be analyzed. On completing his self-analysis, including free association and childhood memories, Freud was intellectually honest enough to publish the dream material in his now-famous *Interpretation of Dreams* (1900).

Later, in the "Dora" case, Freud learned from his therapeutic failure the importance of transference as a resistance and how it could be used as a therapeutic tool if interpreted (Freud 1905a). By 1912, Freud had developed his technique to the point where he was able to deal with acting-out problems and also to guard against transference gratifications by maintaining a therapeutic distance. This in turn lead to the use of the transference neurosis to bring the neurotic conflict directly into the analytic hour (Freud 1912a).

From 1916 to 1923, Freud enlarged his horizon to include the ego and developed the concept that the true function of analysis is the growth of the ego at the expense of the unconscious, followed by the mastery of the id, the superego, and the world of reality (Freud 1923).

In a short period of time Freud developed the theories of psychosexual development, the unconscious, transference, and resistance. Even more remarkably, he demonstrated the need for a personal analysis as part of the training of future analysts and the need for every analyst to detect and deal with countertransference (Freud 1932). Since his data were limited, there were gaps. Those gaps were in part filled in by Freud and his coworkers since then, and more remains to be discovered.

Precisely because psychoanalysis as a philosophy has helped change social mores, the nature of neurosis too has changed. Sex and aggression are no longer taboo behavior. Parental authority is less hypocritical but less sure. Hysterical neurosis is rare now, but neurosis in subtler forms still is pandemic. Its forms are now seen as obsessive symptoms, feelings of alienation and lack of identification, vague feelings of anxiety, psychosomatic symptoms, and open but aimless aggression. These in turn have led to further developments in psychoanalysis to meet the challenge.

To a surprising degree, psychoanalysis and more especially psychoanalytic psychotherapy is a technique that can be applied without accepting all of the tenets of psychoanalytic personality theory. Few psychotherapists, for example, accept Freud's concept of a death instinct (*thanatos*) or a pessimistic view of the human condition. There is, however, much to commend psychoanalytic theory as a *working* hypothesis. Freud's first formulation involved a *topological* approach, of levels of consciousness. Traumas were relegated to the unconscious. Psychoanalysis in its first stage, then, consisted of making the unconscious conscious, releasing both awareness and bottled-up emotion. Another approach was *economic*. Because a human being is a closed energy system, energy that was used to repress unwelcome thoughts into the unconscious would now be available for solving the problems of everyday life. Further experience evolved *structural theory*. Starting again with the unconscious, Freud postulated the construction of the *id*, which is the biological animal nature of man. The id contains psychic energy, *libido*, the expression of bodily urges (*triebe*). The id has no organization or sense of time and obeys the *pleasure principle*, seeking only endless gratification on an amoral basis. Id desires resist change and tolerate without conflict diverse and contradictory feelings. The passionate, violent, lustful feelings seek immediate expression and, if blocked, can be *displaced*, condensed or deflected.

Freud originally postulated that the ego developed from the id: "To prevent excessive stimulation, a special organization has arisen which henceforth acts as an intermediary between the id and the external world. This region of our mental life has been given the name of ego." (Freud 1938) Hartmann, Kris, and Lowenstein (1946) argue more cogently that ego develops from postnatal biological abilities of motility, perception, and memory to handle and adapt to reality. The ego then goes on to incorporate energies of the id, including regression in the service of the ego, which allows it to utilize the creative energies of the unconscious directly.

The ego then perceives the desires and needs of the id and its ability to execute them on the other. It mediates a response and tries to achieve as much of the gratification of the id with as little of the pain of the environment as possible. It seeks to achieve self-preservation at all costs. When the environment is nongratifying, it seeks to change it or to adapt. When stimuli are excessive it utilizes flight or fantasy, or mechanisms of defense (which we will discuss in more detail later). As the observing and reasoning apparatus, even the ego's own behavior can be critically examined.

The identification with and introjection of parental figures serves to differentiate a special part of the ego that Freud called *superego*. The rules and regulations of the superego are broken only at the expense of guilt and anxiety. The ego, when it violates what it ought to do, is forced to modify the behavior or suffer. The self-regarding ego also compares itself to an *ego ideal* based on parental influences. Violations of this level of aspiration lead to feelings of shame, which once again forces the ego to change or deflect behavior (Fenichel 1941).

The Neurotic Conflict

Despite some progress in other kinds of investigation, our best
knowledge of psychoanalysis comes from clinical investigation of
neuroses. Neurosis takes place when an id impulse is blocked from
expression by the ego so that there is no conscious direct expression
or even awareness of the blocking.

The ego and the id battle each other to a standstill, with the
result that the ego is weakened and cannot carry on normal activities. The ego experiences *free-floating* anxiety because the conflict
is unconscious. If the conflict is not contained the weakened ego is
forced to allow some id expression, but to preserve the unconsciousness these expressions are disguised as a compromise between
the wish and the defense against the wish. The symptoms are the
result. The outer world plays a part in that it stimulates one side or
another of the neurotic conflict and thus enters the *intrapsychic*
conflict (id-ego).

The ego defends itself against unwelcome impulses by means of
mechanisms of defense (see A. Freud 1946), which color the nature
of the neurotic conflict. The mechanisms of defense are not in
themselves pathogenic, but become so when resultant anxiety
becomes frequent and painful or the symptoms interfere with life. If
there is a fixation at a lower level of maturation, there will be a
constant tendency to regress when the individual is frustrated at a
higher level.

Superego enters the intrapsychic conflict by making the id wish
unpalatable to the ego through guilt and shame. If the superego is
very severe, even symptoms (disguised and symbolic partial wishes)
cause anxiety, resulting in further blocking of the id and even
greater and painful assaults on the ego.

According to the genetic point of view, the adult neurosis always
has its genesis in the childhood or infantile neurosis. The childhood
neurosis in turn is integral to the child's progression through infancy and his negotiation of maturational stages, from oral through
anal, to genital and the Oedipal complex. The psychic energy of the

libido and the aggressive drives can be invested (*cathexis*) onto a person or thing.

The child begins with a mother who is the provider of instinctual gratification. The mother is therefore the object of the drives and is cathected with both libido and aggression. In the infant's first eighteen months, while the general response is polymorphous perverse, there is primacy on the oral level with the use of the mouth, tongue, and teeth to achieve gratification. Simultaneously, important individuals are incorporated and reality tested through the oral apparatus. Thus the quality of parenting at this level is crucial to the infant's basic sense of security and readiness to give up oral satisfactions for more mature levels. Excessive satisfactions and/or frustrations lead to *fixation* and a reluctance to advance.

When the child advances to the next maturational stage of anal activity, the degree of successful negotiations is already partly determined by the success of the oral phase. As we shall see, if there is a fixation at a lower level of maturation, there will be a constant tendency to regress when the person is frustrated.

The anal phase, with pleasure and aggression in the release and the withholding of feces, has powerful influence on character and ego development, the process of thinking, and the organization of reality testing. Obviously, if toileting is begun too soon the child will perceive this as an excessive demand. This is the first stage at which the child meets the demands of the outside world (in contrast to the oral demands, which are internal). Here are the prime sources for shame.

The phallic phase combines the two previous demands: There is the inner need for genital satisfaction and there is the outside world and its standards of propriety. There is the attracting mother (female) and the denying father (male) to enter into the sexual activity, which now includes pleasure in masturbating, combining touching *and* fantasy.

Every child has his own developmental and temperamental schedule, which may or may not mesh with that of the parents or with those expected from the average child. In each stage there is need for both gratification and frustration on the part of the parent to foster the child's ability to control or release impulses at appropriate times.

A child who has learned from his parents not to worry about being provided with food and/or love, and to manage his sphincters and find sexual gratification without becoming preoccupied with them is mature. Furthermore, he can through the mobilization of libido and assertiveness to new situations master the world ahead of him, create his own identity, and establish his own family. He will be able to relate to others as they really are and take pleasure in giving and receiving love or sex. Finally, he will want to have children and will be able to offer them love and discipline that will enable them to also grow.

If, however, the child was gratified too much or frustrated too much at critical points, neurotic behavior results. On the oral level this can range from nail biting and sarcasm to dependency, profligacy, addiction, depression, and psychosis. On the anal level it can range from the toilet-trained child who regresses to wetting and soiling on the birth of a sibling to the compulsive character, the miser, the disorganized, the workaholic, the obsessive-compulsive, or the paranoid. And on the Oedipal level it can range from the inhibited adult to the hysteric, the Don Juan, the sexually inadequate, or the normal neurotic whose symptoms range from psychosomatic complaints to lack of identity.

Since no individual ever receives optimum genetic potential and parenting, all of us suffer neurotic behavior. As Freud (1930) stated, "Neurosis is the price we pay for civilization." Impulses have to be frustrated from time to time by a body not biologically designed for this amount of frustration; anxiety is the resultant.

The ego has developed mechanisms of defense to deal with these conflicts—they are initiated by anxiety, which acts as a signal so as not to flood the ego with overwhelming pain.

It is by means of the mechanisms of defense (A. Freud 1946) that the ego deals with the id on the prompting of the superego. Two of these mechanisms are basic, in that they are part of all other mechanisms and yet can at times predominate. When the ego feels the signal of anxiety, the processes of regression and repression are brought into play. The behavior is not acceptable on a mature level and will have to be handled on a less mature one (regression), reducing conflict. The conflict will be repressed to avoid anxiety, making it unconscious. However, psychic energy will still be required to maintain it.

The mechanisms of defense are successful if in response to signal anxiety a state of dynamic equilibrium is achieved (homeostasis), allowing for a release of id drives without new signal anxiety. If the balance is not stable and id drives are bottled up, the id energy keeps pressing for release. Further regression takes place, causing more infantile problems. This results in increased guilt and more drastic defenses. Some distorted oblique id drives appear as the ego is weakened by the constant battle. The superego regards even these as anathema, resulting in the ego feeling pain and guilt. This is the neurotic conflict and the disguised id drives are the symptoms. The person is further crippled when blocked id drives are no longer available to power the daily life of the person, resulting in neurotic fatigue.

Finally, the concepts of regression and psychosexual development combined with clinical investigation reveal that the adult neurosis has a nucleus in a childhood neurosis or experience sufficient to cause fixations and disturbance of development.

Psychoanalytic Psychotherapy and Other Therapies

Psychoanalytic psychotherapy is a continuum, of which psychoanalysis is the most intensive. Psychoanalysis attempts to do on an unlimited basis what psychoanalytic psychotherapy strives for on a limited basis. The essential objective of both is the growth of the ego through the analysis of resistance and transference, allowing the ego to solve the unconscious conflicts. The formerly troubled person, now freed of neurotic anxiety, faces the continuing challenges of life on a more mature level, with greater energy and a new sense of identity. Psychoanalysis demands mobilization of all our time and our financial and human resources for an assault on neurotic problems. As in total war, the commitment becomes so intense that the transference itself becomes a neurosis that repeats in essence the nuclear neurotic conflict so that it can be examined, interpreted, and resolved. There are few persons who have the motivation, time, and money for such a protean therapy. The candidates for analysis are first of all professionals who wish themselves to become analysts or therapists. Then come people who have already been helped by intensive psychotherapy and desire to go further. The third group consists of neurotics who are willing to make the sacrifices necessary for psychoanalysis.

Most patients, even many who think of themselves as in "analysis," are really undergoing psychoanalytic psychotherapy. The distinction is not merely one of three or more sessions a week or reclining on the couch. The distinction is based upon an ability of the patient to tolerate over many sessions a situation in which not only is the analyst an unseen, basically reflective person (albeit in a warm emotional setting), but the thoughts and feelings of the patient are regarded as illusions to be questioned, analyzed, and interpreted. While it may be necessary to see the analyst as a real person in the beginning, this too is questioned. The patient must be able to sustain intense anxiety and to tolerate regression without ego damage.

In analysis, part of the ego is encouraged to split off and form a therapeutic alliance with the analyst, while the other part is encouraged to regress to basic instincts and infantile defenses and to confine these reactions to the analyst's office. The patient must further sustain long periods in which the regressive ego experiences object loss and intense loneliness as a re-experience of early conflicts without direct support or reassurance from the analyst. Patients are encouraged to develop access to their "real" feelings and

then must bear the pain of being forced to analyze these same feelings, temporarily depriving them of fantasies, gratifications, and
defenses and piling disappointment on deprivation.

Psychoanalytic psychotherapy, on the other hand, can be
compared to limited war. Psychoanalytic psychotherapy does
demand one or more sessions a week for an extended period of
time. The therapist follows the lead of the patient and to some
extent becomes a real person as well as an object to be transferred
to. Those aspects of the patient's life that need changing to allow
ego growth participate in the transference reactions. Many other
aspects of the patient's life, although neurotic in part, are successful
in the patient's eyes and are not disturbed.

In following the same basic rules, the psychotherapist begins to
interpret from the surface and interprets resistance before content.
Symptoms are not attacked directly. The growth of the ego can be
seen in the degree to which the patient reduces or manages the
anxieties and neurotic problems he faces. Then comes the ability to
free associate and interpret his behavior and dynamics independently of the analyst. The objective is to enable him to carry on the
process in life without the therapist. Thus it is not important that
all the dynamics are uncovered, but that an active, ongoing process
is initiated. If the therapist becomes incorporated as a substitute
figure in the process, this is all to the good because even if only
partially analyzed it is another supportive and helpful neurotic
defensive compromise. In many instances the deeper layers of the
personality are not *directly* analyzed even though therapy is
successful. In some cases the ego grows to the point where a stable
productive equilibrium is achieved, and in others the deeper neurotic conflicts are resolved even though the symbolization and
verbalization are overtly on an Oedipal rather than an anal or oral
level.

The technique of psychoanalytic therapy emphasizes to a greater
degree the use of the nonanalytic techniques of abreaction, suggestion, and manipulation, particularly at the beginning. Unless the

therapeutic alliance becomes very well established, anxiety is rarely allowed to be built up without some resolution by the end of the hour, particularly in once-a-week therapy.

If psychoanalytic psychotherapy is successful, the growth of the ego, instead of leading to a desire for termination, may enhance the psychological horizons to the point where the patient is able to engage in quite deep therapy or then enters formal psychoanalysis. This happens particularly when the choice of therapy is initially dictated by neurotic economic circumstances that are solved by psychotherapy.

As has been stated, the technique of psychoanalytic psychotherapy can be applied with theoretical bases other than psychoanalytic. One such is the interpersonal theory of Harry Stack Sullivan (1953, 1954). Unlike Freud, Sullivan worked primarily with hospitalized patients, and saw himself as a "participant observer," sitting alongside his patient and both looking in the same direction. However, both Freud and Sullivan shared a reluctance to have eye-to-eye contact with patients. Both of them struggled with their own severe personal emotional problems. This led them to have unusual empathy with other troubled humans in emotional distress.

Sullivan saw personality not as the result of intrapsychic forces but as the interchange and interplay of interpersonal relationships under all circumstances. Sullivan conceives of the individual as a "self-system" consisting of the *good me*, the *bad me*, and the *not me*. The *not me* is that portion not recognized because the anxiety would be intolerable. The larger the proportion of *not me*, the greater the neurosis. The self is built up through the approval of "significant others" and operates to preserve a sense of security. Parts of the *self* disapproved of by significant others are blocked from personal awareness but continue to influence behavior. Man pursues security through "power operations." Sullivan's developmental stages begin with mothering in infancy. The learning of language begins in the next stage of childhood, together with the judging of *self* by consensual evaluation (a feeling of security based on a world in which two or more people are linked together by love). In the next juvenile period the child learns to cooperate with his peers and adults other than parents. In preadolescence, development proceeds from egocentricity to social state based on love for a friend of the same sex (another person is as significant as one's own sense of security). Growth from cooperation to collaboration based on sympathy and understanding of others occurs in adolescence, together with genital sexuality.

Logical and coherent thinking is described as *syntaxic;* neurotic behavior based upon the "not me," which is excluded from awareness, is called *parataxic.* This is a parallel to Freudian transference and neurotic behavior.

Sullivan himself practiced a direct approach in which he saw himself as an expert social scientist able to intervene rather directly at times to develop communication in an interpersonal atmosphere. Most contemporary members of his school, as described in a volume by Erwin Singer (1970), utilize the technique of psychoanalysis with a Sullivanian theoretical model in a face-to-face situation. The Interpersonal and Freudian schools have strongly influenced each other and many practitioners are a blend of both.

Erik H. Erikson, probably our most eminent living American psychoanalyst, has also developed a theoretical model of ego development from birth to death. This theory complements and supplements the childhood-centered theories of Freud and Sullivan. They are elegantly described in *Childhood and Society* (1950). The best-known stage, "identity versus role confusion," has become the classic statement of the problems of adolescence.

George D. Goldman and
Donald S. Milman

The Initial Phase of Treatment

Instead of telephoning the therapist himself, John let his wife do it for him. She called to verify the fact that the therapist was the same one she had heard about from a friend. She then requested an appointment for John.

The therapist formed a tentative hypothesis. Either John was resistant to the idea of coming and it was mostly his wife's idea that he seek help, or else he was quite dependent on her and let her do things for him. It was even possible that both inferences had validity.

Take another example. Gerry telephoned the therapist asking whether she could see him immediately because she was so upset. She then asked for, and received, minutely detailed instructions as to how to locate the therapist's office.

In this case the therapist's tentative hypothesis was that Gerry
was in a state of panic, like a lost child. She was ready to surrender
autonomy to an authority figure who would, symbolically, take her
hand and lead her to safety.

Carol presented herself in an entirely different fashion over the
telephone. In a very calm, reasonable tone of voice, she informed
the therapist that she was Pauline's (a former patient's) sister and
she wanted to see the therapist at his convenience.

Here the therapist was struck by Carol's rationality and apparent
psychological stability. Judging by her demeanor over the telephone, her problems were not to be deemed serious. Was she really
that serene? If so, why was she seeking out a therapist? As it turned
out, her control was only a mask covering a great deal of emotional turbulence. Her excessive use of this mask would necessarily
become an important focus of psychotherapeutic treatment.

For these three patients, as with all patients, the initial phase of
treatment had begun before they set foot in the therapist's office.
From the outset, the therapist is making tentative hypotheses about
the patient, and is constantly endeavoring to collect information
that will help to confirm or discard these hypotheses. When the patient actually arrives in the therapist's office, even the way he or
she says hello and takes a seat becomes grist for the therapeutic
mill. For example, a married woman of mature years meets the
therapist in his waiting room, smiles ingratiatingly, and introduces
herself by her first name. She could be telling the therapist that she
is a "good little girl" and wants to be treated as such. If she then
pauses at the threshold of the therapist's office, hesitantly waiting
to be told what to do, she is confirming the "good little girl"
hypothesis.

Once the patient takes a seat in the therapist's office, the initial
interview is "officially" underway. Some therapists use a forty-five-
minute and others a fifty-minute session. During that relatively
short span of time, what happens can set the stage for the ultimate
success or failure of the entire therapeutic enterprise. Therapeutic
errors now can be irremediable. A patient comes to therapy

anxious, depressed, angry, embarrassed, or frightened. Often more than one such emotion is present. People in distress require delicate handling even from friends. In the initial interview, the patient is confronted by a stranger—an unknown, perhaps indiscreet, perhaps incompetent, perhaps even dangerous presence who is supposed to be admitted, on faith, into the patient's vulnerable internal world. How does the therapist chart a course to reduce the possibility of making a disastrous mistake before there is a "bank account" of good will in the patient to draw upon? Some issues related to his problem will now be discussed.

To begin with, how should the therapist comport himself? Obviously, no two therapists will be identical in this respect. Personality differences are inevitably expressed through one's style of being with another human being, whatever the circumstances. Nevertheless, individual style should function within the limits of certain basic principles that define the nature and purpose of the therapeutic relationship. Like a mariner with his compass, the therapist guides himself by these basic principles.

A therapist should never lose sight of the fact that he is being paid a fee for his psychological expertise. This sounds so simple as to be scarcely worth mentioning. Of course the patient expects the therapist to shed light on problems. What could be simpler than that? But the patient also has unconscious needs and expectations deriving from previous significant relationships that are transferred into the current situation and superimposed upon the person of the therapist. Depending on the nature of the patient's early history, she may expect the therapist to be anything from an adversary to an emotional crutch. Moreover, she will unconsciously think and act in such a way as to induce the therapist to play precisely such a role.

Take, for example, the case of the aforementioned female patient who projects the image of a "good little girl" and who unconsciously tries to induce people to be a "good parent" to her. Her behavior is actually likely to produce paternal or maternal feelings in the therapist. It behooves the therapist to be aware of such reactions but not to fall into the trap of acting accordingly. As he keeps in mind the fact that he is being paid to make matters clearer, not to be a "good parent," he reduces the possibility of falling into the trap.

On the other hand, neither does he point out the problem to the patient during the very first interview, before she is ready to perceive, let alone to cope with, an unanticipated problem of such magnitude. That will come later in the therapy, when the time is ripe. For the time being, the therapist adds the item of information to the reservoir of facts and observations he is accumulating about the patient. To be enlightened is the therapist's immediate purpose. Toward that end, he observes, listens, infers, and prudently asks leading questions.

And yet the therapist should not allow caution, at any point during therapy, to render him awkwardly silent, or wooden, or unresponsive, or insensitive. Artificiality has no place in any genuine human relationship. Ideally, a therapist is warm but not effusive; sympathetically accepting but not saccharine; curious but not a prosecuting attorney; impartial but not impassive. Appropriate behavior of this sort, organized to promote the therapist's functioning as a paid expert, will help to protect the therapist from unwittingly seducing or offending a patient. It also serves to remind the therapist that he is not there to entertain the patient, or to become a pal, prospective lover, a fountain of well-meant advice, or a substitute parent, despite any immature wishes the patient might harbor along such lines.

Now, the patient is seated in the chair. The initial interview has begun. The patient has been asked to explain the circumstances that bring her to a therapist. The patient may do so articulately or haltingly, at length or in capsule fashion, calmly or hysterically, finding fault with herself or with others in her current plight. Obviously, there can be no recipe for responding to so many diverse possibilities. There is, however, yet another tried-and-true principle for the therapeutic mariner to guide his ship by.

At any point in therapy, initial or otherwise, watch for indications of resistance and make these the first order of therapeutic business.

Resistance has to do with any inclination on the part of the patient, conscious or not, to oppose changes in the status quo. No patient can be totally without resistance at any stage of psychotherapy. In the early stages, and especially in the initial interview, resistive forces are markedly at work.

Reluctance more often than not permeates the disclosures a patient makes during the very first interview. Events are described in a circuitous or laconic fashion; careful euphemisms are frequently employed; statements are made and then qualified or even taken back; subjects are continually changed; awkward silences punctuate communications. Such are only a few samples of the enormous variety of forms that resistance can take.

Listening carefully, the therapist tries to ascertain from the drift of such discourse just what affect is associated with the manifested resistance. Is the patient embarrassed? Afraid of condemnation? Competitive with authority figures in general? Having identified the affect to his own satisfaction, the therapist ventures to bring the existence of that affect to the patient's attention. If the observation is on target, the patient usually responds with an acknowledgment, and discussion of this problem ensues, hopefully ameliorating at least the immediate intensity of the resistance. In the process, the patient feels "understood" and has acquired additional respect for the therapist's perspicacity. A first step has been taken toward inculcating trust, fortifying hope, and establishing a true working alliance between patient and therapist.

An illustrative example might prove useful at this point. Early in this chapter, reference was made to a patient, John, whose wife telephoned to make an appointment for him. The therapist inferred that John was especially resistive to coming, or unusually dependent on his wife to do things for him, or both.

Encountered in the flesh in the therapist's waiting room, John was found to be a strongly built man in his late thirties who obviously prided himself on keeping his body in tiptop physical condition. The therapist quickly began to amend his tentative hypothesis. There was no dependent-little-boy quality here. Resistive pride most probably accounted for his wife's telephone call. The therapist could visualize him saying to his wife, "I don't want to go. If it bugs you so much, you take the trouble and make the call. I don't want to be bothered with it."

John greeted the therapist with a casual "Hi, Doc" and sauntered, unasked, into the office from the waiting room. His air was one of studied unconcern. He adopted a lounging position in the chair and awaited further developments.

Invited to explain the reason for his visit, John launched into a circumstantial account involving his having an unspecified physical ailment and his wife's being worried about him. Abruptly, he paused and volunteered, "I'm not sure I belong here at all, Doc."

The statement, of course, came as no surprise to the therapist. The patient, however, probably expected the therapist to be surprised and was nonplussed when the therapist took this sudden disclosure in stride. Not only was the therapist gratified that resistance was out in the open, but his "radar system" was picking up vitally important signals. Judging from the patient's tone of voice, from the set of his mouth, from the abrupt movements of his arms, from his sharp, piercing gaze, the therapist realized that he was dealing with a very angry man. Moreover, one could sense intuitively that this man never lived too far from the edge of explosive physical violence.

Bits and pieces of information were beginning to fall into place for the therapist. The patient was a very physical person, proud of his body, and something was ailing that body—something so unpleasant that the patient had pointedly left it unspecified. Barely contained rage boiled below the casual surface, rage having some connection with the unspecified physical problem. His wife was worried about him, probably not only because he was ailing but because she had borne witness to his rage and endured its consequences.

The patient was suffering terribly. A man so heavily invested, emotionally, in what his body can accomplish suddenly finds that this body has "betrayed" him. His sense of identity and self-worth were probably affected. Possibly he perceived his illness, whatever it was, as a form of internal "weakness" that for once he could not eliminate through willpower and exercise.

The illness was the key issue and the patient did not wish to share his pain with a stranger. How to deal with this resistance? Buttressed by his inferred understanding of what the patient must be feeling, the therapist referred back to the patient's physical problem. He said, "It must be very hard on you, with all the care you have taken of your body and all the things you are used to doing with your body, to find that something has gone wrong with it."

The patient responded immediately to the first part of this formulation. He talked about the sports he had played all his life and how he had become a judo expert. Finally, and sadly, he revealed the exact nature of his physical problem. It was of sufficient magnitude to rule out extensive exercise, particularly contact sports. Contact sports, he added, could end up killing him, and he said it in such a way that the therapist realized that the man had seriously considered going out that way, dying with his boots on, so to speak. The therapist ventured this interpretation and the patient ruefully verified it.

The patient and the therapist were by now on the same wave length and communication was flowing relatively smoothly. The therapist by this time had also formulated another tentative hypothesis. A man so passionately devoted to physical prowess and contact sports is not only thereby finding outlet for aggressiveness, self-assertion, and possibly stored-up hostility; he probably is also trying to prove something. What was he trying to prove and to whom?

The therapist now addressed himself to illuminating this area. He raised a question, "Were you always so interested in contact sports and things like judo or did these interests begin at a particular time in your life?"

As a matter of fact, the patient responded, he had not been so completely into athletics until his late teens. Before that time he had trouble when confronted by the prospect of physical violence. Here he paused. Sensing that an important piece of information was about to be disclosed and that the patient was fighting himself about revealing it, the therapist quietly waited to see what would happen. To say anything at this delicate juncture was risky. It could so easily be interpreted by the patient as pressure, which would fortify rather than decrease the inner resistance now in evidence.

Fortunately, in this instance the patient's wish and need to share, and his growing faith in the therapist, overcame his reluctance. He confided that, as a boy and young man, he had suffered bouts of anxiety approaching panic in the face of physical violence. His heart would pound, he perspired profusely, he felt nauseous at such times. But he would force himself to engage in the fight or other activity that was frightening him. By the time he was twenty-five or so, the panic states had been conquered.

The therapist now made an observation that was in essence another question. "Something very important must have happened to you in your late teens . . . something that drove you on to lick the panic problem."

As a matter of fact, the patient said, there was something. It had to do with his father. His father and mother had been divorced for many years and then his father came back into his life when he was perhaps sixteen years old. His father was a physically strong man, an athletic man, a competitive man who twitted him about his alleged weaknesses and egged him on to feats of strength and endurance.

By now the allotted time for the session was almost over and the therapist interrupted to provide the patient with his summary impression and his recommendation.

The patient had been proving to himself and to his father that he was a man. Now that his body would not let him do it any more, he felt like half a man. He oscillated between despair and rage and could scarcely bear to live with himself. "You're right, Doc," he said, "I've got the angries and I don't know where to let it out. I don't want to let it out on my wife and kids." Weekly visits were suggested to work on the problem. A fee was set and a schedule of appointments agreed upon. As the patient left, somewhat comforted and certainly more hopeful than he had been upon his arrival, he paused at the door, turned and said, wonderingly, "You know, Doc, I never told anyone else about how scared I was to fight as a kid. I was too proud to tell anyone." To which the therapist replied, "Maybe it takes just as much guts, or more, to admit when you're scared." The patient smiled and left.

Admittedly, initial interviews do not always proceed so auspiciously, and this is an ideal example, chosen for its exemplary advantages. Still, it has a great deal to teach the fledgling therapist.

The patient's needs and goals and the therapist's objectives were orchestrated to the mutual satisfaction of both parties. How did this come about? The following observations are in order:

1. From first to last the therapist dedicated himself to understanding who and what the patient was as a human being and, secondarily, how he came to be that way.

2. The therapist's earnest commitment to understanding probably registered on the patient, helping him to structure his role in the relationship as well.

3. The therapist never stopped formulating, discarding, and refining hypotheses throughout the communicative exchange.

4. The therapist asked leading questions that were designed to shed light on a particular hypothesis. Sometimes these inquiries were phrased not as questions *per se*, allowing for brief replies, but rather as open-ended statements that encouraged the patient to engage in self-reflective inquiry and "thinking out loud." Spontaneity was thereby fostered but within the structure of the therapist's overall objectives.

5. The therapist was especially attentive to impediments to the

flow of communication; that is, resistance. As much as possible, hypotheses were adduced to account for the probable affect behind such resistance. Therapeutic intervention, when forthcoming, was then worded in such a way as to encourage ventilation of the hypothesized affect. This method fostered the patient's feeling that the therapist understood him.

6. At no time did the therapist venture far from what the patient was feeling and thinking in the *here and now*. No questions were asked regarding his toilet training or whether he had ever had a homosexual experience. The entire process was orchestrated to the patient's current problems, emotions and preoccupations. Digressions from where the patient "is at," to use the popular vernacular, are usually ill-advised in any therapeutic interview, let alone the first. As experienced by a patient, digressions are at best irrelevant or at worst frivolous, if not downright insulting.

7. Before the end of the session, the therapist interrupted the investigative proceedings and took time to make definitive summarizing statements and recommendations to the patient. It was a significant step toward the establishment of a therapeutic working alliance wherein both parties mutually define the patient's immediate *psychological* problem (as opposed to physical problems or external problems like a cantankerous employer), and mutually agree that psychotherapy is the preferred course of action. Psychotherapy, it should be noted, is not always what the occasion calls for. In some cases, institutional care might be the treatment of choice; in others, an extensive program of psychoanalysis, providing that the patient possesses the time, money, and requisite ego strength; in still others, group psychotherapy or marital counseling might be appropriate. The therapist, after assessing the situation to his own satisfaction, offers his honest opinion. If he feels he needs more information in order to make a recommendation, he should say so, delineating the focus of his uncertainty, and invite the patient back for a second exploratory interview to facilitate the eventual mutual decision.

The reader may remember that just before the patient left a fee was set and a schedule of appointments agreed upon. Factors such as fees, appointments, lateness, and payment for broken appointments all fall under the rubric of what Langs (1973) has called "the ground rules of psychotherapy." In the case under discussion, there was no time to spell out all of these ground rules before the end of the first therapeutic hour. Time should be taken to do so as soon as possible, in all likelihood near the beginning of the second therapeutic session. Of course, if a patient returns for the next session obviously in the throes of some powerful emotion, that is dealt with first. Always one discerns where a patient "is at," and acts accordingly. Sooner or later, though, the ground rules need to be defined.

Patients and therapists often "act out" some problem in living when it comes to setting and paying fees. One married woman, still dependent on her mother, told the therapist that her mother would be paying the fee and he was to send the bill to her. The therapist pointed out that she herself had already complained that her mother still ran her life. Was it wise for the therapist to further this state of affairs by sending her mother the bill? It was at least her responsibility to receive each month's statement. Afterward, she could handle the money problem herself in any way she chose.

Some patients attempt to get the therapist to lower his fee, not because they are really so short of funds but because of some psychological reason. One patient might need to confirm her self-image as a businessperson who drives a hard bargain; another wants to feel like "a special child." It behooves a therapist to take these possibilities into consideration before agreeing to lower fees.

Therapists also have been known to act inappropriately in terms of fees. Some lower fees because of a compulsive need to feel or to be seen as "the nice guy," others because they doubt their own worth as professional practitioners. Some therapists do just the opposite and raise their fees too much or too often, possibly in a pseudo-sibling competition with the therapist down the street who just raised his. The point is that money is loaded with symbolic power beyond its actual value as a medium of exchange. Small wonder that it is so frequently misused, emotionally, in or out of the therapeutic situation. Many therapists tell patients that they will send out a bill on the first of the month and will expect payment by the tenth. When payment is not forthcoming, the delay could be construed as a form of resistance calling for therapeutic investigation.

A therapy session is usually forty-five or fifty minutes in length, depending on the practice of the individual therapist. The patient should be told this in the initial session so he knows what to expect in terms of time. He is also told that, when and if he comes late, the session will end on time nonetheless. A therapist's schedule is such that it can be no other way. Patients follow each other at predetermined times with little or no margin for error. Habitual latecomers are also acting out some form of resistance that has to be explored therapeutically—perhaps it is defiance, or a masochistic bid for punishment, or perhaps it is for some other reason.

Vacations also come under the ground rules. Some therapists tell their patients when they are going on vacation, in August, let us say, and expect the patients to take a vacation at the same time. Suppose a patient objects that she cannot arrange a vacation in August; her employer insists that she take her vacation in July: Is she expected to pay for her missed sessions in July while she is on vacation and also for her missed sessions in August while the therapist is on vacation? Obviously a great deal of ill will could be generated over issues like this, so they should be clarified at the inception of treatment. Some therapists are arbitrary, setting all the rules and expecting patients to abide by those rules. Others prefer to be more flexible and work out individual arrangements, at least in certain circumstances such as those described above. Whatever the case, the therapist is supposed to be watching for signs of resistance in which the patient is possibly avoiding sessions by not trying sincerely to have the two vacations coincide.

Missed sessions present an analogous problem. Most therapists charge for all broken appointments routinely; otherwise it becomes a relatively easy matter for patients to skip an appointment whenever their resistance dictates that they are "too tired," or "not feeling well," or that they simply had to pick their Aunt Mathilda up at the train station precisely when they were supposed to be in the therapist's office.

The initial interview is a finite entity with a beginning and an end. No such certainty exists regarding the termination of the initial phase of psychotherapy. Most therapists would probably agree that the initial phase has moved into the middle phase when certain conditions are met:

1. The patient perceives the therapist as someone trustworthy and competent who can assist her to solve specified (and, by implication, the as yet unspecified) psychological problems that the patient recognizes. Along with this perception, the patient should have developed toward the therapist an emotional attachment of some magnitude and durability. To put this idea another way, the patient has begun to be *in transference* to the therapist.

2. The patient is clearly aware that her problems are not all external; that is, she realizes that she makes significant contributions in some fashion to whatever her plight happens to be. Her perceptions of these contributions can and probably will vary—both in terms of scope and the relative importance she accords to each—as psychotherapy proceeds. Her understanding and psychological vision will both broaden as time goes on. But when she has defined for herself even one aspect of her being that she wants to change in order to facilitate her growth as a person, then she is entering the next phase of therapy.

3. The patient has implicitly entered into a contract with the therapist, a working alliance in which both parties are consciously dedicated to exploring and explaining the patient's psychological world in terms of her personal life history.

Upon the fulfilment of these three conditions, the patient has become a patient in spirit as well as name. Hypothetically, this can occur within a single therapeutic session. Usually it takes longer. But all such demarcations are merely artificial boundary lines, conceptualizations having little or no impact upon real life. One might as fruitlessly ask where youth ends and middle age begins. Each day is an adventure, the beginning of the rest of one's life. The dictum applies equally well to the process we call psychotherapy.

Lorelle Saretsky

Transference

The task at hand is to focus on the varied and frequently tumultuous aspects of transference during the course of psychoanalytic psychotherapy. The relationship between patient and therapist, although limited by personality dimensions of each, is characterized by a deepening and intensified involvement. This chapter will endeavor to parallel this escalating interaction by focusing first on extratransferential manifestations, next on the general transference positions (positive and negative), and finally on specific transferential reactions.

Transference is a complex phenomenon that is rather awkward to define. As a verb, *to transfer* can be equated with *to generalize*. The concept of generalization is a familiar one in learning theory (Dollard and Miller 1950). The term implies that any of a variety of similar stimuli may evoke the "same" response, even though the response has been habitually associated with only one of these stimuli. This principle of generalization applies to any kind of response, whether cognitive, physiological, or behavioral. *Transference* as a noun emphasizes "something" that is transferred. In psychoanalytic theory it is not always clear what that something is, although most people agree it seems to be a feeling or an emotion.

It is generally acknowledged that all of us carry residuals of past experiences that create a stylistic pattern of reacting in particular situations to particular people. These patterns are repetitive and become, at times, inappropriate and disruptive to the individual. The impetus for the behavior, the transferential reaction, is unconscious and tends to narrow perception, empathy, and self-awareness.

Transference has been variously defined, but most contemporary psychotherapists understand it in terms of those feelings and attitudes that were originally experienced with regard to significant others in the past but that are now displaced or projected upon the therapist. In therapy, the patient repeats in the treatment relationship the characteristic responses and expectations he has developed over the course of his life; the perception of the therapist at these times is a distortion. The patient lives through memories as though they were something real existing in the present. These revivals and anachronisms are reproductions in miniature of past interactions that cannot as yet be remembered.

Transference manifestations are so valuable in the psychotherapeutic setting because they give the patient a remarkable opportunity to re-experience all varieties and mixtures of feelings that cannot be recollected. The patient expresses in action what has been forgotten and repressed. He repeats a past experience unconsciously, without knowing that he is repeating it. This compulsion to repeat colors the patient's functioning in all facets of his life, and in fact forms the basis for his coming into treatment in the first place. The patient is responding inappropriately not only to the therapist but to other significant figures and situations in his life. The therapy session provides a framework for the patient to be confronted with all his past stages of object relationships. The format of therapy is conducive to temporary, circumscribed regressions so that the patient can slowly observe his typical way of coping with the different developmental phases that he has passed through.

At one time or another, treatment offers the opportunity to explore the need for symbiotic closeness; the fear of loss of love; ambivalent feelings; the experience of hate and sadism; the loss of control; the anxiety of being controlled; feelings of self-sufficiency, sharing, and competition; sexual strivings; and the establishment of an ego identity. As each of these themes are discussed, the regressive nature of transference reactions will rekindle a reenactment of earlier dramas, enabling the therapist and the patient to reconstruct accurately what went wrong in the past and to work through toward more effective solutions in the present.

What is there that is unique to the analytic process that evokes this regressive reenactment of early developmental dilemmas?

1. The generally permissive and encouraging attitude of the therapist allows the patient to let his deeply hidden feelings and impulses come to the fore.

2. The technique of free association and having the patient lie on the couch combines with the permissive climate to facilitate an intensification of primitive feelings. Expressions of forbidden incestuous striving and tabooed impulses (for example, oral, anal) can saturate the therapeutic hour with the vivid reliving of primitive, infantile affects.

3. The patient's knowledge that it is the therapist's function to help him to abandon and renunciate his infantile wishes would naturally resurrect deeply hidden negative feelings toward parental figures, who at one time were also agents opposed to his infantile desires.

4. Finally, the deliberately induced mysteries surrounding the analyst (authority, anonymity, silence) induce a feeling of awe that the patient presumably experienced in his childhood relations with his parents.

These combined factors are believed to bring about a relatively unhampered resurgence of instinctual tendencies and attitudes—a new version of the original childhood neurosis.

In the less intensive situation of psychoanalytically oriented psychotherapy, the transferential manifestations are somewhat reduced. The patient is seen less frequently and usually sits up and talks face to face with the therapist. The general tenure of the session is more anecdotal, reality bound, and problem oriented, and less involved with fantasy and imagery. Nevertheless, dreams, associations, and avoidance or continuity of the thread of the prior session lead the patient and therapist to transference behavior.

A patient whom I see on a twice-a-week basis seemed to alter her approach to the treatment process on a rather regular weekly basis. For two sessions she would associate freely, display a curiosity about the meaning of her thinking and behavior, and draw perceptive and thoughtful conclusions about her own psychological functioning. The following week, she would spend most of her sessions asking me "Why?" and seeking reassurance that she would some day be "OK." When I became aware of this pattern and pointed it out to her, we traced its genesis to her reliance upon her mother's predictions, which held magical connotations for her: "Mother will always know what you were doing, you can't fool me." "Mother's the only one who knows what to do and what's best for you." These exhortations were at once terrifying and comforting. When independently exploring and interpreting her own behavioral determinants, feelings of anxiety were elicited that could only be quelled by projecting the quality of magical seer/mother onto the therapist, which she did in the subsequent sessions.

Since the historical aspects of psychoanalysis—a discussion of which must include the key concept of transference—has been discussed elsewhere in this volume, I will limit my inclusion of history to a brief overview.

In 1909, Freud was invited to receive an honorary degree at Clark University in Massachusetts by its president, Dr. G. Stanley Hall. He delivered five rather extemporaneous lectures there, which were formally written in 1910. The fifth lecture concerned itself with resistance and transference. Freud stated that in every psychoanalytic treatment of the neurotic patient, the phenomenon of transference occurs. The feelings of affection that are directed toward the physician, according to Freud, have no basis in reality, but are traced back to old wishful fantasies of the patient, which have become unconscious.

Negative transference was dismissed as a resistance by Freud in 1912, while positive transference was held to be the therapist's ally in treatment. Later, however (1915, 1916–1917), Freud suggested the necessity of understanding all transferential responses for cure. The special interest of the patient in the doctor, rather than in the resolution of his own conflicts, mandates the analysis of the transference as resistance.

The distinction between positive and negative transference has been muted by some theorists who have deviated from the classical frame of reference. Wilhelm Reich (1949), in fact, understood all positive transference as reformulations of negative feelings: "Positive transference . . . drown out such rudiments of genuine object love as have not yet been consumed by the neurosis. They are in themselves results of the neurotic process, in that the frustration of love has given rise to hatred, narcissism, and guilt feelings. They are sufficient to keep the patient in analysis until such time as they can be dissolved; but if they are not unmasked in time, they will provide the patient with strong motives for breaking off the analysis." (1949, p. 121) The transference in Reich's view was a maneuver consistent with the patient's character defenses and served as a resistence to change.

Henry Stack Sullivan (1954) formulated a vocabulary and point of view different from Freud's. An instance in which the words are different but the concept is similar is found in the Sullivanian theory of parataxic distortion as it manifests itself in the analytic situation. According to Sullivan, parataxic distortion is the greatest pitfall to communication between two people in that there is an "illusory me-you" pattern that is instituted. In therapy, the parataxic mode, facilitated by anxiety, repression, and immaturity, transforms the therapist into an illusory personification. The distortions, however, are an oblique attempt to communicate some need. The therapist must expect, recognize, and deal with these parataxic distortions as they arise in treatment. In this instance, therefore, we can see the parallel between the "transference" in the Freudian sense and "parataxic distortion" in the Sullivanian paradigm.

Freida Fromm Reichman (1950) conceptualized the positive transference as a security operation of the patient with the therapist. She felt that a genuine affection for the analyst can set in only after the patient has been really helped and that early verbalizations of admiration are a distortion of reality and, indeed, may be likely to function as a disguise for negative feelings. Fromm Reichman advocated discouragement of the patient's attempts to discuss feelings toward the therapist other than those feelings relating to the understanding and resolution of the patient's problems.

Erik Erikson (1950) tended to stress the importance of mutuality as vital to cure in the therapy situation. His goal was not to foster the transference in order to gain insight into psychic distortions, but rather to encourage equality between patient and therapist. The relationship should be one "in which the observer who has learned to observe himself teaches the observed to become self-observing." (Freedman et al., 1975) This view is very different from that taken by another current clinician-theorist, Hyman Spotnitz (1976), who utilizes special techniques deliberately to facilitate the mobilization of negative, aggressivized attitudes during the analytic hour.

There has been renewed interest in this country recently in the work of Melanie Klein (1882–1960). The Kleinian concepts are directed toward an instinct-oriented approach in contrast to the interpersonal, culturally determined precepts. Transference interpretations provide the bulwark of the analytic process in the Kleinian view. The interpretations are of primitive fantasies residing in the deepest unconscious of the patient. Klein (1952) postulates that the transference originates in the earliest object relations and that the expression of aggression, love, hate, envy, guilt, and anxiety derive from universal innate positions of infancy and early childhood. The mechanisms of these early positions have been utilized to broaden the understanding of current ego psychologists, particularly in their work with severe borderline and narcissistic character pathologies. The individuals who fall into the latter diagnostic categories had been considered unanalyzable by Freud because he believed that a transference could not be effected. Current theoreticians, however, have clarified the unique, but certainly available, transferential reactions of the more severely disturbed patient.

Extra Transferential Issues

The patient comes into treatment seeking competent professional help with the problems at hand. The patient expects, and rightfully so, that the clinician will help to effect some change in his or her life. Simply to say that much, of course, obliterates the latent transferential properties of the patient's expectations, but we shall put that aside for the moment and deal only with the establishment of the therapeutic alliance, which is a necessary but not sufficient component of a "successful" treatment. In order to create the alliance an educative process must unfold. The patient needs to know what is expected in the situation—that is, to free associate, to listen to oneself, and to be open to exploration of possibly painful motives, perceptions, characteristic trends, and so on. To do so with another implies a capacity for trust and relatedness. One must be capable of consciously thwarting and analyzing what can be a compelling desire to behave with hostile aggression, sexual activity, or total passive receptivity. The sincere cooperation of the patient lies in the ability to delay gratification, tolerate frustration, and control behavior. Talking, not acting out, is the keynote of the psychotherapy. A therapeutic alliance implies that patient and therapist have the same goal—to understand. When that intent is accepted and adopted, the alliance is established. The patient's "observing ego" joins the analyst's "analyzing ego" in a common inquiry.

An adolescent girl with whom I worked entered therapy with the stance characteristic of her interaction with all adults, that is, silly, secretive, and provocative. Lynne's presenting problems concerned her poor social relationships, in which she was frequently scapegoated by her peers, and her failing scholastic work in school. Lynne, during sessions, would often giggle inappropriately. I asked her several times during early sessions why she was laughing and she usually said, "I don't know." After about a month, when rapport and trust had begun to be established, Lynne responded independently to her laughter. She told me how foolish she felt when, "the dopey sound comes out of me at the wrong times. Maybe if we talk about when I do it, I can understand and I won't have to keep on with it." Lynne then began to talk freely about sexuality, a topic heretofore avoided.

This particular anecdote was selected because I believe it illustrates the rather complicated relationship in psychotherapy. The patient must be able to see the psychotherapist as different from others in the environment in a positive sense; that is, he must have trust in the nonjudgmental interest of the analyst so that the "bad" thoughts and feelings need not be censored. At the same time, the therapist is the reservoir for similarities, real and distorted, to past and present persons in the patient's life. The ability to negotiate the swings in perception begin after rapport is established and is successful to the degree that both parties are capable of relating to each other. All too often, in the literature, the onus is placed upon the patient, but the analysts too are limited by their own personalities. Analysts need to be able to respect the patients, to value the patients as fellow human beings, to be committed to the patients' well-being, and to be interested in the patients. Therefore, although a therapeutic alliance is necessary to the analysis, we have to back-track and discuss the "real relationship" between patient and psy-chotherapist.

Greenson (1967) uses the term *real* to refer to the realistic and genuine relationship between patient and analyst. "Transference re-actions are unrealistic and inappropriate but they are genuine; truly felt. The working alliance is realistic and appropriate, but it is an artifact of the treatment situation. In both, the real relationship is genuine and real." (p. 217) Core qualities of the analyst are per-ceived and strengthened through validation.

> A patient whom I saw on a once-a-week basis maintained an attitude of the "good analytic patient" in terms of preserving my anonymity. He was a therapist himself and had a "set" for the proprieties of the patient/analyst interaction. He rarely asked questions about my personal life and if he chanced to express curiosity about me he would preface his question with, "I know you can't tell me, but. . . ." Of course, there were many distor-tions in his perception of my personal life. As we understood the basis for these distortions in terms of past relationships, he was able to conclude, and rightfully so, that I was somewhat reserved and that he had artfully blended this characteristic of me into an idealized image of my "professionalism" and "analytic stance."

> The "real" part of me, a reserved quality, was sifted out of the myriad of patient/therapist interactions as an integral characteristic that was, indeed, accurately perceived by the patient.

The Transference Neurosis

Psychoanalytic treatment does not create transference reactions: it merely brings them to life by facilitating their development. Every-one has transference predispositions; the unique manifestations that are evoked by the particular patient-therapist interaction are called the *transference neurosis*. Freud (1905*a*, 1914*a*) gave this phenomenon such a designation in order to characterize the replacement of the everyday symptoms of the patient's illness by the creation of a new illness within the analytic situation. If a climate is established in which the repetition compulsion will thrive, the patient's neurosis is admitted "into the transference as a playground in which it is allowed to expand in almost complete freedom and in which it is expected to display to us everything in the way of pathogenic instincts that is hidden in the patient's mind." (Freud 1914*a*, p. 154)

The therapist tries to take stock of any factor within her control that would contaminate or curtail the burgeoning of this process. This would include a heightened sensitivity to any intrusion, value, or countertransferential reaction that would make it difficult to make the clear distinction between the patient's infantile projections and his realistic reactions to the stimulus value of the therapist. Among the conflicts within the therapist that can contaminate the transference neurosis, the following are most common:

1. Neurotic attitudes toward money

2. Difficulties related to sex; the expression of hostility and assertiveness

3. Perfectionistic impulses that push patients toward goals beyond their capacities

4. Narcissistic needs for admiration

5. An impatience with frustration and failure

In order to bring about the maximal development of transference neurosis, the following techniques are employed (Wolberg 1954, p. 401):

1. Employing passivity, anonymity, and opaqueness in the relationship

2. Focusing discussions on other than present life situations

3. Using free association in the couch position

4. Concentrating on dreams and fantasies

5. Breaking down repressions by seeing the patient several times a week

6. Avoiding dealing with unrealistic attitudes toward the therapist until these have built up to overwhelming proportions

7. Acting a role that coordinates with that assumed by the traumatizing parent

8. Taking compassionate, accepting, nonjudgmental attitudes

9. Avoiding need gratification; setting of limits (fifty-minute hour, fee schedule)

10. Repeatedly interpreting resistances

Quite early in his career, Freud (1912a) recognized that because the nature of the original relationship that is transferred onto the present is more or less infantile, all transference manifestations are essentially ambivalent. Nevertheless, he found it useful to break transference down into its positive and negative aspects. The term *positive transference* Freud reserved for feelings toward the analyst of love, fondness, trust, concern, admiration, respect, and so on.

Freud originally saw positive transference as a reflection of the nonpathological aspects of the personality. He advocated that the therapist ally herself with this healthy aspect of the individual, and the positive transference would then become the analyst's strongest ally in a struggle with the patient's pathological facets. Over a period of time, Freud came to modify this position somewhat. He began to see the patient's "transference love" as a source of resistance that may oppose the work of analysis. The patient's perception of the therapist may rest on an anticipation of a loving, indulgent, all-giving mother. So long as the honeymoon period prevails and this attitude is not frustrated, the patient is appreciative, cooperative, and feels loved. When the therapist is later viewed as making demands of her own, being strict or punitive, the infatuation can turn into stubbornness, defiance and withholding.

An obsessional woman with whom I worked began treatment with a respectful, affectively positive attitude toward me. As therapy progressed, she reported that she "woke myself up during the night to indulge in sexual fantasies about you" (her sexual relationships have always been heterosexual). The exploration of this behavior led to a recapturing of early memories that had been repressed. When the patient was three, her mother suffered a miscarriage and because of complications was told that she could not bear any more children. That event heralded a severe depression that never fully lifted. The abrupt cessation of mother's loving availability created a nostalgic longing for the lost, "early" mother. The sexuality that was acted out with her boyfriend was a transformation of the frustrated wish to be held, stroked, and tenderly caressed by the mother she had lost at age three—that part of the mother that she had forgotten ever existed.

Positive transference should not be confused with the idealized transference. In its extreme form, it is usually associated with the severely narcissistic patient. The therapist is perceived as the perfect, grandiose reflection of the patient's idealized self or idealized object. Left alone, the image will shatter into an equally extreme devalued, disparaged sense of the analyst, another reflection of the self that the patient endeavors to deny.

Jack, a successful performer, had a multitude of social and sexual contacts, nevertheless, he had not one true friend. He was distant, unrelated, and uncaring about the people in his life. His manipulative compliments to me became crystallized into an idealized transference. I was "the best" because, of course, he expected himself to have nothing but the best. He bolstered his point of view by collecting validation from others—others whom he began to see were carefully chosen for consensus. As I challenged his narrow and distorted view of me, he began to criticize my low self-esteem, my refusal to "accept anything at face value," my contrariness. In a span of weeks, I fell from being the greatest to a lowly position of total ineptness. Nevertheless, Jack was able to continue in treatment and during the next phase, I became a "nonperson" to him. He claimed to have no feeling about me "one way or another" and just came to the sessions "to work on myself, for a change." Of course, I was no different from all the people he knew in his life—just a sounding board, but of no real consequence to him. Through dreams, repeated reflection of his insulation to protect his grandiose self from that punitive, self-denigrating self, culminated in a more integrative and synthesized view of himself and others. People, myself included, became "real" to him, instead of objects to be "handled and used."

As the term suggests, negative transference refers to a patient's negative attitude toward the therapist. The negative transference may be expressed as suspicion, fear, anger, hostility, aversion, contempt, loathing, bitterness, envy, competition, and so on. It is always present in treatment although it is much more difficult to uncover than the manifestations of the positive transference.

The appearance of negative transference reactions early in treatment, before a reliable working alliance is established, tempts the patient to act out and break off the therapy. In order to forestall such a development, the analyst persistently tries to interpret these trends before they begin to significantly sabotage the course of treatment. Once a positive relationship has been firmly established, however, the negative transference is indicative that the patient is comfortable enough to relive hostility and hatred to early childhood figures in the transference. This is a necessary phase of every successful analysis.

An interesting instance of negative transference emerged during the treatment of a couple. Their presenting complaint was of frequent, rageful battles about the parents of each. Both Fred and Cindy "hated" their in-laws. Both protected their own parents and quarrels would take place with a compulsive regularity on an almost daily basis. After several months in therapy, the couple began to behave lovingly and playfully with each other during sessions. They had difficulty reporting what they had fought

about during the week with any affective involvement, and indeed, did not fight the day of our once-a-week session, nor did
they quarrel the prior or subsequent day. They had become
united in their criticism of me. They predicted what I might say
before the session, processed and picked apart what I had said
during the session, and, in some collusive fashion, made the best
of what they saw as the worst in me. Fred and Cindy both
needed some "parent" figure to hate in order to love. There was a
see-saw effect of feelings—someone had to be "down" in order
for another to be "up." This was traced to the history of their
early lives. Each had a parent who felt loved by the child and
who could love in return only if the child was drawn into the
position of ally against the other parent. The child was deprived
of the opportunity to express love to both parents in spite of
flaws; they had had to make a choice. When the couple projected
their "bad parent" onto me, it served to deflect their negativism
from the "bad in-law/parent," to unite them in a common cause
without the need to protect and defend their real parent, and it
freed them to be more loving toward each other.

Some patients' energies are largely diverted toward verbally
attacking, frustrating, and provoking the therapist. This aggressivized transference is based on both genetic and current displace-
ments, defenses against current unconscious fantasies and self-
directed rage, and direct anger. It is often accompanied by impaired
judgment, marginally defective reality testing, fluid self-boundaries,
and primitivized superego derivatives (projection of self-criticisms).
As Langs (1973) has indicated, the presence of these often intractable negative reactions constitutes a serious disruption of the therapeutic alliance and a potential threat to the entire therapy. At the
same time, they can represent a crucial form of communication
from the patient, but they must be transmitted to the patient in a
manageable form if treatment is to succeed.

In my experience with aggressive transference reactions, there was
one particularly threatening incidence of it in ongoing private

psychotherapy. The patient was a young college student, who had been a social isolate for most of his life. Having experienced the pain of being a scapegoat during his early school years, he developed an interest in body building. He was tall, somewhat overweight, and muscular. He effected a menacing manner that warded off potential friends as well as foes. He was a virtual reservoir of suppressed rage, which was apparent the very first session. I anticipated that I could become the transferential object of the amorphous, free-floating, long-standing unneutralized aggression. I laid down the "ground rules" that he could say whatever he pleased, in whatever tone of voice he chose, but he could not get up from his chair during a session. Once, during an especially vituperative outburst, he got out of his seat, paused briefly, said "Oops, I'm sorry," sat down, and continued his verbal attack on me. The structure offered this patient a chance to express the anger he had squelched for years while providing a safety valve in terms of limit setting so that he knew that he "was not allowed," as he put it, to really hurt me.

Certain kinds of patients develop an intense sexualized transference love. Their desires are compelling, insatiable, and unrealistic. Freud came to the conclusion (1915) that this type of positive transference must be understood as anything but positive. Rather than advancing therapy it retards progress and is therefore a manifestation of resistance. Analysis is hindered because the patient tries to exclusively gratify his needs through the therapist, cannot tolerate surrogates, and makes the need satisfaction an end in itself rather than a subject for analysis. Such patients often succeed in defeating the therapist by making the analytic stance ineffectual, a combination of the perceived inadequacy, impotence, and uselessness of the people in the world around them. This negative transference masquerading as a positive attachment must be dealt with as one would deal with any other manifestation of resistance—by analyzing, not by withdrawing. However, if not confronted early in its development, the eroticized transference may flourish with such tenacity that its counterproductive hold on treatment will become intractable. The patient then will have to be referred elsewhere.

During the course of psychotherapy, some patients will act out their transference reactions instead of reporting them in words and feelings. They may be acted out toward the analyst or outside the analysis toward others. Some illustrations of acting out are precipitously quitting a job, having an affair, delaying payment of fees, forgetting an appointment, and so on. To substitute recollection for repetition and to free the patient from compulsion are the ultimate goals of the therapist's efforts. The therapist persistently attempts to keep the patient aware of this goal and directed toward its accomplishment. The patient is instructed not to carry his impulses into action and, especially, to delay any important decisions that would significantly affect his life until they have been discussed first. The clinician tries to take advantage of every opportunity to help the patient to replace deeds with words. Every transgression of this prohibition is identified as a resistance and is explored during the analytic hour.

The rule against acting out (Freud 1914a) provides the therapist with a lever by which to reveal the patient's resistance, poor impulse control, and infantile behavior. Each violation of the limits exposes the patient to his unwillingness or inability to cooperate with the therapist for the achievement of the rational goals of the treatment. "Each renunciation of action in favor of thought and words advances the analysis and the patient's progress toward maturity." (Greenacre 1950)

Acting out was the hallmark of JoAnn's behavior when she entered treatment. She drank too much, was promiscuous, and stole with persistent regularity. These behaviors became controllable as JoAnn began to pursue her underlying motivations and to verbalize them. She began to get closer to people in the "outside" world as I mentioned that it was important to raise issues about herself and me as they occurred to her. Several weeks after I made this statement, JoAnn came into the session visibly shaken. She had had her only homosexual experience and felt "disgusted and disturbed." Exploring the impetus for the behavior led JoAnn into a difficult "confession" of having known that a homesexual gesture toward her was intended by my earlier remark. She was "too ashamed to respond to it. I felt I would handle it when you made some physical advance."

This patient eroticized and sexually acted out in all of her interpersonal relationships. In treatment, too, my invitation to verbalize was misconstrued as an invitation to sexual play. She acted out this "demand" with another woman and, in fact, replayed a role familiar to her; that of the beautiful, exploited sex object. JoAnn was nicknamed "Gorgeous" by her parents, who used her as their showpiece. Her feelings, intellectual capacity, and artistic talents were unnoticed at best, and more usually thwarted. As she grew up, JoAnn treated herself in a similar manner. She thought of herself as "a great body" and as "a terrific face." The terror of the emptiness beneath the shell was what brought JoAnn into therapy. The expectancy of exploitation, transformed from the demand to be a showpiece as a child to being a sexual object as an adult, was introduced into the therapy where it could be understood and worked through.

Occasionally, the therapist who is working with severely disturbed individuals will experience very primitive transference phenomena. These transient regressive reactions to the therapist most often reflect a breakdown of the observing ego's capacity to test reality adequately.

A patient asked me if I had to go to the bathroom. When she was asked what made her think of this, the patient replied, "Because I have to go." This same patient constantly pleaded for physical contact and became very upset when frustrated. She insisted that I feed her, and when I refused she became violently abusive and hysterical, accusing me of "not acting like my mother. You are my mother, so act like my mother."

In this case illustration, we see the fluidity of the subjective/objective dichotomy. The patient's assumption that if she had to go to the bathroom so must the therapist; that if she wanted to be fed or held the analyst must gratify her, was a recreation of infantile omnipotence. This patient operated from a conviction that the therapist was really her mother. The deterioration of organized, differentiating ego faculties created a loss of distance. This trend is in contradistinction to the neurotic patient who knows the therapist is not his parent and, even if he momentarily reacts as though the analyst were his parent, is able to employ his intellectual awareness to snap back to reality.

To conclude, it is apparent that issues regarding transference are merely touched on in this chapter; it is a vast and encompassing concept. When the therapist notices a reaction or an overreaction that is unwarranted and subjective, it can be concluded that this is a transferential manifestation. However, there are those who hold that all strong feelings, even outside the therapy setting, are transference, including love. It may seem rather disconcerting to think that the person with whom one is in love is merely one upon whom we can displace and project lovable qualities. Is the beloved an ego-ideal equivalent? It is a debatable point.

Marvin Daniels

Resistance

The word *resistance* summons up a multitude of meanings for the psychoanalytic therapist. It refers to any inclination, idea, feeling, attitude, or action—anything at all the patient does, consciously or not—that fosters the status quo and impedes personal growth.

Obviously, there can be uncomplicated forms of conscious resistance: for example, the patient deliberately does not disclose significant information. There are also uncomplicated forms of unconscious resistance: for example, the patient forgets appointments. For the most part, however, expressions of resistance are not only unconscious but also quite complex, difficult to detect, and still more difficult to explain to the mutual satisfaction of patient and therapist.

Many, if not most, patients do not believe that resistance exists, at least not for them. Why should I pay fancy prices, they argue, to oppose my own progress? They have not yet arrived at the understanding that resistance is not confined to the therapeutic arena. It is, rather, an inescapable property of the human condition. Personal growth defines itself in its struggle against internal resistances just as light defines itself against a backdrop of darkness. One cannot even be conceived without the other.

For a more complete appreciation of what resistance means to the psychoanalytic therapist, it is useful to adopt an historical perspective. The thoughtful reader will then perceive that psychoanalytic progress was also—and just as inevitably—accompanied by the "labor pains" of one or another aspect of resistance.

Freud's earliest formulation regarding neurosis involved the notion of conflict. His patients had certain sexual urges and ideas that they could not tolerate in themselves (internal conflict). To put the matter another way, these people were *resisting* facets of their own sexuality. Their solution was to repress the reprehensible desire with its associated mental contents, a step that frequently culminated in the eruption of a neurotic symptom.

From the start, then, Freud had to contend with, and be inspired by, the challenge of resistance. Not long after his first major publication on dreams (1900), he observed that psychoanalytic treatment is fundamentally a problem of re-education in which patients learn to overcome their own internal resistances (1905b).

In this new method, how were resistances to be dealt with? No longer was repression to be attacked head on through hypnosis. Instead, the focus was on early childhood fantasies, experiences, and parental attitudes that gave rise to repression. In time, adult understanding supplanted childish apprehensions still haunting the deeper layers of the mind. Repression thus lost its motive power, and memories were permitted back into consciousness.

Toward this end, the therapist was to be on a constant alert for indications of resistance—blushing, verbal hesitation, changing the subject, and so forth. The mental content behind such signs was like the reverse of Ariadne's thread, leading not out of the labyrinth but into its very heart, where the Minotaur of magnified childish terrors was waiting to be encountered. And the goal was not to kill but to "tame" the Minotaur through understanding. Unless this happened, there could be little or no lasting progress.

Resistance does not, however, begin and end with the concept of repression. In describing "transference" (1912a, 1915) and the "repetition compulsion" (1914a), Freud made the point that resistance inheres in those phenomena as well.

The concept of positive and negative transference is thoroughly explained in Chapter 3. For our immediate purpose, it is well to bear in mind that since transferences receive emotional impetus from the past, they lend themselves to excessive and inappropriate reactions. In fact, whenever we find ourselves unduly aroused by an apparently minor event, we have reason to suspect that a transference has been at work.

Take the example of a male patient who flew into a rage while describing a mix-up with theatre tickets. He had wanted tickets for a certain Saturday night, and he wrote to the theatre requesting them. Unfortunately, all seats were sold out for that night, and the manager of the theatre took it upon himself to send tickets for another Saturday. But the patient could not use the tickets on that date—he had a previous engagement. There was reason to be vexed, true, but he was more than vexed; he was beside himself. With ringing imprecations, he denounced the manager; and the more he carried on, the angrier he seemed to get.

A therapist has to know when *not* to intervene as well as when to say something. This therapist held his peace, awaiting further developments that he hoped would shed some light on what was happening.

At last, and in the very midst of the tirade, the patient abruptly exclaimed, "Just like my father—giving me what *he* wanted instead of what *I* wanted!"

Immediately his anger subsided as he realized that his passion had little to do, really, with theatre tickets. Now he recalled how once, as a boy, he asked his father for a baseball glove. The father had refused. Times were hard, baseball was frivolous, and money was scarce. Later the father changed his mind and decided to surprise his son by bringing home the glove. Knowing nothing about baseball, he went out shopping for a bargain and found a catcher's mitt, useless to his son who played second base. He brought a box home and his delighted son tore it open—only to find a catcher's mitt. He tried to explain his disappointment to his father. Now hurt and disappointed himself, his father counter-attacked. The glove was a bargain. The boy was an ingrate. It was the catcher's mitt or nothing! Inside himself, the boy hurled defiance back at his father. Rather than settle for less than what he wanted, he would take nothing. Or, rather, he would get where he wanted to go on his own, pitting himself against limitations, scorning half measures and the half-a-loaf, asking for help only at the point of direst extremity. He had grown up living by such principles; they constituted the warp and woof of his character structure, permeating all of his dealings with the world at large. It was not a single incident that led to an entire way of being for this man. The incident of the catcher's mitt was only a sample from memory, epitomizing the chronic mutual misunderstandings and disappointments that existed on both sides of the father-son relationship. Events like this produced an ultimate sense of futility at the core of the growing boy; and the futility had to be defeated daily by the inwardly defiant, self-sufficient mode of being he defined for himself through his character traits.

The problem of coping therapeutically with such "character transference," as Wilhelm Reich (1928, 1929) was disposed to call it, will be touched upon again before this chapter ends. In the meantime a point should not be overlooked. Any situation containing crucial components paralleling one's past can elicit extreme feelings, negative or positive, even when the target personage is, like the theatre manager, unknown and unseen. All of us are doomed to repeat vital childhood experiences endlessly (the repetition compulsion). Instead of recollecting, we "act out" the essence of the germinal events. It is a primary therapeutic objective to unmask the disguised connections between the present and the past.

Resistance usually obscures the perception of one's transferences and repetition compulsions. The patient simply insists that the past has nothing to do with present-day reality. For example, a female patient may think she has fallen madly in love with her male therapist (positive transference). An immediate therapeutic goal is to weaken repression and facilitate memory of similar but long-forgotten feelings about her father. The therapist does not confront her directly with this interpretation. If he committed such a therapeutic error, she would become justifiably angry and her resistance would increase sharply. She would maintain heatedly that the very idea of having a sexual interest in her father is absurd, if not downright disgusting.

Let us suppose that matters proceed auspiciously and the repression lifts. She now remembers a sexual interest in her father and competitive feelings toward her mother. Does this mean that she quickly loses her passionate attachment to her therapist? Not necessarily. There is a desire to bring to fruition with the therapist what could not be accomplished with father. After all, there is no incest barrier between her and the therapist. So she might well fall back upon another line of resistance. Yes, she admits, once she loved her father sexually, but that has no bearing on her current love. Her therapist she loves for himself alone (although, in reality, she knows next to nothing about him, about his private, inner self). She dismisses the obvious objection that, logically speaking, she has contrived to fall in love with a phantom of her own imagination.

Insistently, the therapist declines to become involved and directs the patient's attention to the irrationality of her behavior. In many cases the proclamations of love eventually change to a torrent of abuse. Negative transference has replaced the positive.

But who is the underlying target of this negative transference, father or mother? The answer usually depends on whether the patient feels wanted but thwarted or simply unwanted. If she thinks herself unwanted, probably she saw her father as rejecting. She is now relating to the therapist in a negative father transference. On the other hand, if she is convinced the therapist secretly loves her but withholds himself, then she feels thwarted. The therapist has come to represent mother who stood in the way.

Let it be noted, parenthetically, that rapid transference changes are not uncommon in psychotherapy. Transferences are mainly dictated by the patient's emotional needs, not by the reality of the therapist's age or sex.

Many a therapeutic venture has foundered on the reefs of intense transferences. Our hypothetical female patient, frustrated and angry, might well consider discontinuing treatment, especially if her childhood resolution to the "Oedipal triangle" was to withdraw, emotionally, from her parents. In so doing, she would be, in effect, acting out a repetition compulsion. The therapist would try to anticipate her behavior and head it off through the judicious use of interpretation. Success in this endeavor is contingent upon several factors, including the timing and wording of the interpretations. Basically, however, success or failure with any patient, in any context, is related to the patient's overall mental health. As in everything else, the more resources the patient brings to a project, the more he or she is likely to profit from the experience.

Stormy transferences can also occur in homosexual patients (males with male therapists, females with females) and in male patients with female therapists. Whatever the case, the therapist's goals remain essentially the same: to dissolve repressions; to encourage the ability to distinguish between fact and transferential distortions; and to enable the patient to live more realistically in accordance with achieved insights. Psychoanalytic therapy thus addresses itself not merely to changes in outward behavior, but to changes based on expanded memory, increased self-awareness, and enlightened choice.

Nonetheless, the therapist expects to encounter obstinate resistance every step of the way. If and when repressions are overcome, a patient might still minimize, or deny, or try to rationalize into ineffectuality whatever has been accomplished. Here the so-called defense mechanisms of the ego frequently come into action, denial and rationalization being two such defense mechanisms. There are others. Later in this chapter, the issue of defense mechanisms will be accorded more detailed attention.

Let us assume for the moment, however, that the influx of new resistances is also overcome. The patient now realizes how drastically the past affects the present. It is no longer a matter of merely giving lipservice to an idea she once read in a book. The impact can be staggering. How many perceptions have been distorted! How many important relationships have suffered! How much work has to be done to correct one's failings! Why it's like trying to cut down a whole forest with a hatchet! The prospect is intimidating and generates new resistance.

Not only that. Sooner or later the patient comes to the additional realization that everyone else is in the same boat as she. Parents, spouses, lovers, friends—all living out transferences and repetition compulsions with her and with each other. She induces others to play allotted roles in the drama of her repetition compulsions. Simultaneously they are inducing her to play an allotted role in their dramas, and none of the players is aware that old scripts are being repeatedly acted out with minor variations. It's worse than a play by Pirandello! Throw up your hands! Why bother?

Let us suppose that temporary despair resolves itself and the patient is ready for the next phase of therapy. There is another discouraging discovery. Repetition compulsions do not vanish with awareness of their existence. The past hangs on stubbornly. It must be caught in the act, so to speak, again and again, mulled over and renounced afresh in the light of new memories and deeper understandings. Such *working through*, as Freud coined the term for it (1914*a*), distinguishes the analytic method from many other forms of psychotherapy. The task is arduous, difficult, often painful; but the road to maturity is always rocky.

A patient named Mary Solberg wrote a poignant, hitherto unpublished poem that distills the problem into its essence:

> My mother's gone into hiding
> behind you.
> Your motives are agonizing replays
> of mine, in search of mother
> behind me.
> I can see the shadow of her martyred smile,
> longsuffering, knowing, pained,
> and hear the echo of her voice.
> You should know better
> (and so, dear God, should I, so should I).
> We take such trouble to copyright
> our own translations of the same ancient texts,
> you'd think we'd written them ourselves.
> But no, we only spend ourselves
> trying to come up with that one new word
> that will change the meaning just enough
> to make a difference.

Freud's next contribution to the theory of resistance involved *adhesiveness of the libido*, a term that appeared in his *Introductory Lectures* (1916–1917).

Now Freud had speculated that people differ innately in ways that predispose them to particular difficulties. Constitutional weaknesses in given organ systems could, for example, give rise to specific psychosomatic symptoms. Why does one person suffer from migraine headaches while another channels emotional stress through the gastrointestinal system? Perhaps, Freud thought, there was an interaction between the exact nature of the emotional conflict and the innate strength or weakness of the organ systems in the body available for discharge of conflictual energies.

Similarly, Freud proposed that libido varied in its constitutional strength and in its mode of operation from individual to individual. Libido is sexual energy that is the fuel for many components of mental functioning. During early childhood, libido was believed to build up to a high level (cathexis) at various erogenous bodily zones—oral, anal, phallic—rendering these zones intensely excitable when cathected. Stimulation of a cathected zone yielded much physical pleasure. Freud theorized that, in some people, libido was quite mobile, moving readily from zone to zone. In others, perhaps, it was sluggish, tending to "adhere" to specific erogenous zones and the love object choices associated with those zones.

Most modern practitioners of psychoanalytic therapy have reservations regarding the pragmatic value of this theory. Freud occupied himself on two fronts—helping people, and creating a theoretical system of such broad scope that it could eventually encompass and explain every aspect of human behavior. At times his efforts in the latter domain resulted in conclusions that are difficult if not impossible to test scientifically. Libidinal adhesiveness falls into this category. So too does Freud's concept of the "death instinct" (1920), which posits an innate striving in living material to return to a preorganic state of things. Despite criticism from within and without the psychoanalytic movement, Freud never relinquished his belief in the existence of and adverse effects of libidinal adhesiveness and the death instinct on the course of psychoanalytic therapy (1937, 1938).

In *The Ego and the Id* (1923), Freud took a momentous step, discarding the "topographic" approach. To take its place, he devised a different frame of reference, "structural" theory, which involved the concepts of id, ego, and superego. The entire problem of resistances now had to be re-evaluated within the framework of structural theory. Freud set himself to this task in *Inhibitions, Symptoms and Anxiety* (1926), where he traced resistances to their sources in the id, or the ego, or the superego, those three basic components of the total psychic apparatus.

Repressions and transference phenomena (including the repetition compulsions) resulted from the ego's attempts to master anxiety. Libidinal adhesiveness and its consequences were forms of resistance from the id.

Freud also now described a type of resistance attributable to the superego. Some people, he said, need to suffer because suffering represents unconsciously desired punishment. They are victims of their own superego, unaware of the reason for the vague but pervasive sense of wrongdoing that afflicts them. Many of the people who "can't stand prosperity" fall into this category. Success evokes foreboding instead of pleasure, as though there were to be a penalty for sinning. They lead joyless lives. Obviously, in the therapist's office the threat of success would arouse the same resistance it arouses elsewhere.

Uncovering the reason for the guilt is the therapeutic goal. A sixteen-year-old boy named Jay is a case in point. He was brought for psychotherapy by his parents because of failure to achieve up to his potential at school. Exploration revealed, however, a more fundamental problem: he led a drab and colorless life. His sole pleasure was trout fishing, a solitary pursuit for him.

Whenever Jay became proficient at something, he gave up either the progress or the activity. Each September he started well at school. His performance always deteriorated long before June. He took piano lessons and stopped just as he was showing signs of real progress. The same thing happened when he took up tennis.

The fly in Jay's ointment, as it turned out, was his father. Ostensibly, father wanted closeness with his son. What he really wanted, unconsciously, was competition. When Jay found an activity that interested him—piano, tennis—his father joined him in taking lessons. Even schoolwork was not a private preserve; father enjoyed "discussing" it with him. Interestingly enough, father hated trout fishing, the one pursuit for which Jay's enthusiasm never flagged.

Jay was reluctant to face the unpleasant fact that his father was using "togetherness" as an excuse to compete with him. Delicate questioning, however, at last elicited corroborative memories: surpassing father on the tennis court, or at the piano, and wincing at the sight of father's crestfallen face.

He could not refuse to play when father insisted. To refuse would have hurt him. His alternatives were to allow father to excel or to give up the activity. Each time he kept his self-respect and dropped the activity. At school he sincerely wanted to produce. Father's capable academic record had been made known, and he was expected to match it. Or was he? Jay suspected that his father had very mixed feelings in this regard. So he stopped trying.

To Jay, then, success meant hurting his father, and his superego rebuked him severely for that, a process culminating in his ego's decision to relinquish the "forbidden fruit" of success. Further therapeutic investigation uncovered links between these recent events and an Oedipal competition with father for the love of his mother. All children, however, have to navigate through the choppy, dangerous waters of the "Oedipal triangle," coming to grief therein only when blown about by unfavorable circumstances. In Jay's case, the unfavorable circumstance was his father's chronic competitiveness. Wishing to supplant father in mother's loving arms is already an ultra-risky situation for any little boy. Having a father who competes back is usually more than a small boy can handle at that stage of development. A permanent problem is likely to ensue. In Jay's case, fortunately, a deeper understanding of the nature of the problem ultimately freed him from the tyranny of his superego.

Freud discussed another type of resistance in his *Inhibitions, Symptoms and Anxiety* (1926). He called it the *secondary gain* of the ego. The idea had far-reaching implications that were scarcely appreciated at the time.

What is secondary gain? A person is in conflict with herself. Her ego finally decides on a mode of behavior, neurotic or otherwise, that appears to be a compromise solution. But the ego often does not stop there; it takes a second step, leading to the so-called secondary gain. The ego talks itself into regarding the new behavior as being not merely necessary but laudable. It does this in the interest of maintaining its inner self-consistency and self-image. Such action is a universal propensity of the human ego. Thus, a psychotherapist often discovers that a given patient's first line of resistance is the secondary gain, which the ego now regards as a pleasurable asset.

Take an illustrative example. A fifteen-year-old girl is brought for psychotherapy. On a deep unconscious level, she is afraid of her sexual impulses. Fear of sex is converted into a symbolic equivalent: fear of "germs" and of "contamination." Now she does not have to acknowledge to herself her real concerns, which are distasteful to her. Concomitantly, she has provided herself with a "reasonable" excuse to keep her contact with boys superficial.

In order to eliminate the possibility of contamination, however, she engages in ritualistic practices that irritate and antagonize members of her family. She inspects dishes and silverware minutely. She complains of her brother's toilet habits. She insists on brushing off the seat of the car before she sits in it. Moreover, she staunchly defends her actions. Brought to a therapist, she informs him that she tries her very best to keep the members of her family from falling prey to disease, but they haven't the good sense to appreciate her noble efforts. What began as an inconvenient symptom is now a badge of honor. Such is the nature of the secondary gain.

The real issue here has to do with setting up a *working alliance* between therapist and patient. When both agree regarding the goals of treatment and the ground rules of the investigation, there is a working alliance. Establishing a working alliance is relatively easy when the patient brings to the therapist's office a problem she wants to get rid of—that is, an *ego-alien* problem. An actor, for example, finds himself immobilized by recurrent stage fright. He can no longer perform and he is desperate. His problem is very ego-alien. On the other hand, behavior acceptable to a person's ego is termed *egosyntonic*. What is egosyntonic to us might constitute an enormous problem to everyone else but it does not bother us.

Therefore, we have little incentive to change our egosyntonic behavior.

There is an axiom in psychoanalytic therapy. That which is egosyntonic has to become ego-alien to make therapeutic progress possible. So easy to say, so hard to accomplish. Probably more failures occur in this type of therapeutic enterprise than in any other. Tamper with the egosyntonic and the human ego generally bristles with defense mechanisms like a porcupine.

Prior to 1926, Freud discussed a number of the ego's mechanisms of defense. His daughter Anna later wrote an entire book on the subject (1946). Only some of the more common defense mechanisms will be described here.

Rationalization is a defense mechanism. The girl who was afraid of germs used it. When we say that someone is rationalizing, we mean that he or she is justifying, excusing, and defending conduct from internal as well as external criticism. The rationalizer uses some variety of false logic to trick everyone concerned, including herself. As Kenneth A. Fisher once observed, "Nothing is harder to penetrate than a person's self-deception." (1976, p. 190)

Projection is another defense mechanism. In projection, we unconsciously attribute our undesired qualities to others, then roundly attack them for allegedly possessing those same attributes. Actually, they have now become convenient targets for our own self-hatred. A simple example would be the man who accidentally breaks something valuable and snarls at the nearest innocent bystander, "Just see what your silly whistling made me do!" Note the element of persecution in the complaint. By its very nature, projection lends itself to feelings of persecution. In psychotherapy, a patient might "accuse" the therapist, silently or otherwise, of having the very same "weaknesses" that she detests in herself, and for which she expects to be judged and condemned by the therapist. If she can, to her own satisfaction, discredit the "judge," she has nothing more to fear. When a patient criticizes a therapist for some supposed malfeasance, such as being selfish, the chances are good that she is saying more about herself than about the therapist. But in so doing, she is also implicitly relying on an old military adage: the best defense is a good offense.

The defense mechanism of *denial* amounts to a simple refusal to accept adverse evidence. It is analogous to the behavior of a small child who spills his milk on the rug, looks fearfully at his mother, and says, "I didn't do it, I didn't do it." The child is not really lying. In terror, he is hoping that the words will somehow have the magic power to obliterate the incident and its possible unfortunate consequences.

Denial in psychotherapy is more sophisticated but no less redolent of magic in its obstinate insistence on minimizing or avoiding undesirable facts. A female patient of adult years reported dreaming that her therapist was reclining with her on the analytic couch. Head on his shoulder in an intimate position, she carried on her analysis. But she denied any possibility that the dream image was sexually suggestive or implied any romantic thoughts whatsoever.

A patient unable to acknowledge feelings for a therapist is likely to displace these feelings, positive or negative, on to some substitute who stands for the therapist in the patient's unconscious mind. The woman just discussed could well fall wildly in love with someone bearing a superficial resemblance to the therapist. Unless the therapist can persuade her to examine her motives, therapy might end prematurely on the grounds that she now has someone else to confide in.

Hostility can also be displaced from one object to another. A punished child, unable to strike back at his parents, vents his spleen on the family dog. He, too, is displacing.

The defense mechanism of *isolation* provides an interesting contrast to denial. Isolation means denying little and acknowledging much, but the acknowledgment is like a desiccated mummy—a statement of intellectual fact with all the emotional life gone out of it. A male patient reported admiring his nubile sister and abruptly finding himself with an erection in her presence. "How did you feel about that?" asks his therapist. "I didn't feel anything about it," he replies. "Did you perhaps feel embarrassed, annoyed at yourself, annoyed at her, eager to leave the room, eager to stay in the room—what?" The patient is genuinely puzzled. "I don't know," he says. "I just know that I was sexually aroused." The therapeutic goal here is to help the patient to learn to restore connections between his thoughts and the affects that are supposed to go with those thoughts.

A more thorough account of all of the mechanisms of defense can be found elsewhere (A. Freud 1946; Fenichel 1945). Suffice it to say that any or all of them might be used by any given patient to render ideas and actions more ego-syntonic and thus less amenable to psychotherapy. To go one step further, within the therapy situation the human ego has at its disposal, and in the service of resistance if it so chooses, all of the resources, capacities, and skills available to it in everyday life. Erudition, intelligence, imaginativeness, sensitivity, humor—all of the ego's assets could be marshaled at any given time to defend the status quo.

On the other hand, there is, hopefully, a portion of this same ego that, allied with the therapist, opposes the status quo. It is relatively objective, self-scrutinizing, and dedicated to growing as a person. It should also be fortified by positive transference, which provides for an essential minimum of belief in therapy and the therapist.

To the working alliance the therapist commits all of his own ego assets, tempered by the humility that comes with experience.

Authentic therapy emerges only if the doctor can hit upon a true way of being with the patient, a way that is not solemnly helpful, or a way of making money and being important, or a way of satisfying his need for dominance and potency. This genuineness employs nascent skills—sensitivity and imagination and compassion—which are aroused by the problems and nature of the particular patient. This true therapy is novel and it can happen but once. The next patient, or the next day, requires something else. (Fisher 1976, p. 168)

Closely related to the problems of secondary gain and the ego-syntonic are the characterological resistances. A person's character traits are ego-syntonic by definition, and comprise a person's dominant, habitual mode of dealing with the world inside and outside herself. An individual's character structure obviously has enormous survival value; otherwise it would not have come into existence. It is so tough and enduring that Reich dubbed it the "character armor" within the total personality (1928). But when characterological predispositions are too one-sided and inflexible, there are two outstanding consequences. First, the character armor persistently creates its own pitfalls and frictions in the course of daily living. Second, it eliminates the possibility of further personal growth: one is confined as well as protected by one's own armor.

There comes to mind an exceptionally successful businessman in his forties who sought psychotherapy at his wife's behest. They were on the verge of separating, and he was desperately unhappy. With tears in his eyes, he pleaded for help and said that he would cooperate in any way possible to avert divorce. But his characterological dedication to competitiveness threatened to defeat his conscious purpose from the very outset of therapy. In a short time he brought in the following dream.

In the dream, he was playing tennis. A crowd was watching, his wife among them. His opponent was a neighbor with a formidable serve, and he was competing under conditions of maximum disadvantage: he had no racket with which to hit the ball back! He was acutely aware of his wife's eyes upon him. He wanted to impress her. It occurred to him that the only way to win the game was to induce his opponent to serve out of bounds. Yet that had to be done inconspicuously and in a sporting manner.

The neighbor with the racket stood for the therapist. Actually, the therapist and the patient were neighbors, at least in the sense that they resided in the same community. As used in the dream, the words "serve" and "racket" both had double meanings. Psychotherapists are members of a service profession. Unlike dentists, chiropractors, or physicians, however, they do nothing to a patient.

Unlike lawyers, they carry on no activities on behalf of a client. Instead, they sit and talk, occasionally offering what they hope will be useful observations. If one were ill-disposed toward psychotherapy, one could declare that a psychotherapist is little better than a "racketeer"—which is what the patient was saying, pictorially, in the dream image.

Furthermore, the patient unconsciously conceived of the relationship not as a joint enterprise with a common goal but as a form of competition with a winner and a loser. For him, all relationships with other men were fundamentally competitive; his character structure allowed for nothing else. And in this particular competition the patient saw himself as an inevitable loser. The therapist was in a position to serve (make interpretations). That position was inherently superior and therefore intolerable to the patient. Every interpretation made by the therapist was regarded as a "put down." How could he compete under such adverse circumstances? Yet there was a solution: subtly and inconspicuously to inveigle the therapist into making faulty interpretations (serving out of bounds). His unconscious intention was to do just that. He had to defeat the therapist at all costs—even if it cost him his marriage.

The dream was discussed with the patient. His self-defeating plan of operation was nipped in the bud. His competitiveness became the subject for a great deal of therapeutic investigation. Much attention was ultimately accorded to his relationship with his father, the first competitor with whom he felt himself to be at a distinct disadvantage.

Resistance often is manifested in dreams long before the patient is aware that she harbors any resistive inclinations. Sometimes the patient even resists the interpretation of a resistance dream. In such a case, the therapist bides his time and collects the evidence, waiting for the appropriate moment to bring it up again. From the dream the therapist often can infer what form the resistance is likely to take. Knowing what to look for, he detects much that he might otherwise overlook.

A sixteen-year-old underachiever who came willingly for psychotherapy, consciously eager to cooperate, provides another example
of unconscious resistance depicted in a dream. After a few therapeutic sessions, this young man was asked to lie on the couch and
engage in free association. He complied with no apparent reluctance
but, that very night, he had the following dream.

In the dream, he was on the way to school in a little handmade
wooden automobile, the type used by children in soapbox derbies.
It had no motor, and he was being pushed up a steep hill by his
mother. The image of his feet sticking up in front of him seemed
important or, at least, pictorially vivid. Classmates were passing
him by, in real automobiles and under their own power. He envied
and resented them. Yet the thought did not even occur to him to
get up and walk. He simply stayed put and let his mother push. He
knew that eventually they would reach the top of the hill and then
he would coast down until the little automobile ran out of momen-
tum. Sooner or later his mother would arrive and push him again.
There the dream ended.

Lying on the couch, he finished reporting the dream and his
therapist quietly said, "Look at your feet sticking up at the other
end of the couch." The effect was instantaneous. The patient
realized immediately that the soapbox automobile stood for the
couch, and his mother stood for the therapist. To put matters
somewhat more accurately, he had begun to relate to the therapist
in terms of mother transference from the moment he lay down on
the therapeutic couch. He had intended, unconsciously, to treat the
therapist as he treated his mother. He would be childishly passive,
dependent, and lacking in initiative, productive only if and when
"pushed" by the therapist. Now his resistive inclinations were, at
least, out in the open, and exploration began of the unconscious
collusion between him and his mother. Unconsciously, she had a
need to infantilize him. Unconsciously, he acceded to her wish
despite what it did to his self-esteem to sit in a symbolic baby
carriage and watch his peers pass him by.

In conclusion, several points are worthy of emphasis:

One. The psychotherapist who promises quick psychological "cures" of a far-reaching nature is either ignorant of, or deliberately ignoring, the omnipresence of resistance. Shun him. There is no shortcut to maturity.

Two. The therapeutic enterprise resembles art more than science. It is full of quirks, novelties, and unexpected developments as in any act of creation. Each unique individual elicits an element of uniqueness from the therapist, and so the process cannot be reduced to a cut-and-dried scientific regimen.

Three. There is no personal growth without some inner pain. In growing, we must relinquish—or at least modify—treasured aspects of ourselves: our self-protective devices, our self-deceptions, our irrational passions, our prides, our prejudices, our self-pity. Giving them up means feeling exposed to danger and being at risk, an unfamiliar self in a newly unfamiliar world.

Four. Personal growth forges itself out of the eternal dualities inherent in all of us: for example, consciousness versus unconsciousness, love versus hate, order versus chaos, past versus future, passion versus reason, to name but a few. Inevitably our polarities interact, and resistance is the inevitable accompaniment to the internal struggle. This perspective enables us to understand, *au fond*, that true growing requires as much hell as heaven.

Hitherto unpublished, the following poem, written by a disciple of the late Swiss psychiatrist Carl Gustav Jung, speaks volumes on the subject within the space of a few lines.

Growing

The hell I know has human eyes
Angels that are demon-wise
        Pain to beauty, beauty's pain
        Rounded wisdom round again
Love comes down in hate's disguise.

Life it is that never dies
Love it is that tries and tries
      Child and devil, devil's child
      Innocent and running wild
Stropped for seizing heaven's prize.

When hell is selling, heaven buys
When hell is telling, heaven lies
      We struggle dreaming struggle's dreams—
      And reaching where our wisdom gleams
The child within us cries and cries.

                         —A.O.

Ruth-Jean Eisenbud

Countertransference: The Therapist's Turn on the Couch

Some ten psychoanalytically oriented therapists, psychologists, and social workers meet informally for conversation and colloquium. Their evening begins with the question by a senior member, "Am I the same self in the office as I am out of the office?" Some of the group respond emphatically, "the same"; others decisively, "a different self." Close discussion of the dialectical nature of these positions brings them to a common middle ground. When it comes to countertransferences, the private self has won over the professional self.

In the course of this chapter, we review how in many ways the private self is an integral part of the professional self, and how the therapist must perceptively rectify and surmount ("work through") countertransferences in attaining effective therapeutic behavior.

Much of this presentation is garnered from years of an evolving research and conceptualization of countertransference by many different writers. The text references are chosen to indicate key sources of the borrowed material, and to invite the reader into further exploration of the theory and lively history of this important aspect of psychoanalysis.

Countertransference is of concern because it blocks both the patient and the therapist. As we shall see, it also sometimes facilitates the patient, and it is always a tool in the therapist's hands.

The term "counter" in the word countertransference is confusing, as it seems to refer to opposition to transference. It refers instead to responses in the therapist that are like the patient's, as in the word counterpart. Between therapist and patient, as in a chess game, the countertransference, the pieces on the side of black, are the analogue, the replica, the counterpart of the white pieces. As in a chess game, unlike in the game of checkers, the counters on both sides are many and varied. When we are dealing with a particular response, we should properly refer to *a* countertransference, not to *the* countertransference.

In a wider sense, countertransference is present in all human relations, as is transference. Our natural responses to one another are complementary. The term countertransference is often used now, even in psychoanalytic discussion, to designate all kinds of relatedness to the patient. In other than Freudian orientations, such as interpersonal or existential, the term is used, advisedly, simply to mean a responsive reaction in the therapist to the patient. In this chapter, the psychoanalytic technical meaning will be used. Countertransference (CT as we shall designate it) refers to the emotional process present in the therapist when it is (1) in relationship to the patient, (2) has a bearing on the therapeutic process, (3) involves unconscious feelings of the therapist, (4) has a component of conscious or unconscious anxiety, and (5) represents a blending of appropriate, defensive, and fixated responses.

CT can make the therapist's responses inappropriate, highly changeable, and ambivalent. Often it is on the basic oral level, as is the patient's transference, and this entails childish dependency and a high degree of hostility. As such, CT has been called "patient vectors in the analyst." CT in the therapist allows a minimum of plasticity of character. She becomes rigid in response to the patient and cannot allow the patient time to thaw out nor the diversity of option that makes for change. Indeed, a CT on very partial perception of the patient often identifies the patient as a significant figure in the therapist's past.

CT also includes affective, supportive reactions, verbally and nonverbally supplying therapeutic warmth and trust. Nonetheless, useful or restricting, CT denied will blind the therapist to various aspects of the patient.

Because of the patient's influence on the therapist's unconscious feeling, self-analysis, as Freud early discovered, is an imperative. When self-analysis fails, the therapist should turn for help to a colleague and/or seek further personal therapy.

Some Causes of CT

As a first cause, there are many *social and situational pressures* in the therapist's life outside of treatment that influence unconscious response to a particular patient in treatment. For one, in the course of training, the young therapist is aware of official evaluation and consequently reacts emotionally to the patient who is resisting or acting out and defeating therapy. The young therapist may feel on trial with a supervisor; practicum and internship entail serious investment of effort, time, and money, and all this depends on a patient's remaining in treatment and making progress. CT may be reflected by an impulse to gratify and thus bribe the patient to stay in treatment. Sometimes the therapist has the illusion that every case must be cured and that every real therapist is a magic healer. Under such pressure, failure is experienced as a personal humiliation.

Trainees are often engaged in personal therapy or personal analysis and love or hatred spills over from their personal treatment. Positive or negative identification with their own therapists leads them to aspire to perfection and be tense and exacting or to compensate for the frustration in their own treatments by gratification of their patients. Sometimes to fulfill the role of a competent professional, a therapist clings to ritual and rigid rules and suppresses self-awareness and intuition. If the patient's welfare seems a personal, heavy responsibility, guilt and fear of failure may attend the therapist.

In like manner, social and situational factors influence experienced therapists when they feel the pressure of maintaining a reputation with peers or entertain omnipotent fantasies engendered by a continued isolation. Moreover, established therapists often have emotional investment in proving a particular orientation and a standard of living for self and family to maintain. When they are training younger therapists, their perceptions of and tales about the senior therapist make part of the lore of the land and the group evaluation threatens the senior's image. Confidentiality may easily become a matter of too much concern in that case, and enter as a CT into the treatment of the younger therapist.

Many CTs would seem far less mysterious to therapists if they would be willing to consider the simple story of where they are coming from in a given session. Angry words left unsaid in a quarrel outside the office, concern over the illness of someone very close to them, a near accident on the way to work, even physical pain are situational pressures that can spill over into their responses, just as such pressures influence responses on the Thematic Apperception Test.

Unresolved, neurotic problems of the therapist are our second cause, and form the core of CT. For example, projections of early introjected significant people from the therapist's past unconsciously define responses to the patient.

A woman therapist unconsciously experienced her woman patient as she had a younger delinquent sister, whose antisocial "cool" and rebelliousness she hated and envied. As an elder sister, the therapist had identified with her "poor mother" in deep involvement with her sister's difficulties, and in anxious maternal concern. Uncharacteristically, the therapist found herself distant and unaffected when her young patient expressed despair. Such coldness on her part was ego-alien to her, and she explored her failure of empathy with her supervisor. She found that unconsciously she was refusing sympathy this time round as if her patient were her sister, and refusing, this time, to become maternally involved. Moreover, she felt that it was her turn now, like her sister (and like her patient as she perceived her), to remain self-involved. She was engaged in an unresolved struggle against identification with her masochistic mother. This time, instead of being overconcerned, she even felt glad of her patient's bad luck and distress. Because such sadistic pleasure had to be repressed, she responded with cold aloofness.

Unresolved neurotic conflicts such as these are a matter for individual insight. The therapist herself has the clearest access to a personal conflict and its strength; it is usually all too familiar from self-analysis and/or from work done in personal therapy. As with transference, a general description of the many neurotic conflicts aroused in CT would entail a review of the dynamics of personality.

Communication of a patient's state of being is a third cause of CT. In some way the patient communicates anxiety or sexual arousal directly to the therapist. Taking the clue from the patient, the therapist becomes trapped in unconsciously identifying with the patient. For example, verbal and nonverbal clues of tension in an expressive, anxious patient create diffused anxiety and even depression in the therapist. Although this kind of patient is somehow contagious to others as well as the therapist, among therapists such seduction will affect one more than another. A therapist whose traumatic past has brought her to overreaction to danger and alarm is so affected. Perhaps an hysterical parent in the therapist's past or a severe illness in the family have given rise to this morbid sensitivity. A CT then grows of protectiveness and caution. The therapist fears imminent psychosis or violence, and in its service works for repression rather than against repression in the therapy. It is an observed regularity that anxious material brings anxious responses. At such times the therapist needs to pull back into her own skin, so to speak, and avoid CT anxiety, even at the cost of temporarily withdrawing empathy.

A patient's romantic and erotic yearnings are sometimes as contagious as anxiety, and a male therapist can be aware of erection or a female therapist of a rush of desire. Temporary, sudden breakthroughs of "real" erotic CT in a close, intimate proximity, although more self-evident, are not nearly as disturbing to the treatment as neurotic defenses raised against such feelings. (Indeed, accepted and managed, these feelings may add to the beauty of scenes.) One defense against lust takes the form of the classic male projection, a righteous anger with a woman for seduction, as Adam said in regard to Eve, "The woman gave it me and I did eat." In classic manner a woman therapist defensively withdraws to cold, dignified unresponsiveness from a man patient when his confession of passionate, sexual feelings arouses her. She will not be "reduced" to a "sex object." Male or female therapists can defensively interpret the patient's sexual feelings when they experience them as seduction, or as a "power fight."

Another common defensive reaction is an attempt to diffuse instinct with intellectualization. The therapist then systematically interprets sex as a pre-Oedipal need for closeness or tenderness or as an expression of warmth in order to deny the instinctual sexual or Oedipal involvement of herself or her patients.

Although sometimes contagious, transference love from the patient more often supplies unconscious narcissistic flattery than arousal. We are often reminded of Freud's (1915) dry comment that the patient's "falling in love" is "induced by the analytic situation and is not to be ascribed to the charms of his person." Today we would add or of her person either, for she, too, as therapist must "lay not such flattering unction to her soul."

It is sometimes equally hard not to take the patient's hate with self-reference. To be consistently an object of fear, hatred, and critical complaint arouses CT feelings of self-protective aggression. The patient who persistently calls for advice and reassurance as evidence of interest and competency on the part of the therapist wounds the therapist's self-esteem. Feelings in the therapist of narcissistic injury and hurt personal feelings are much more likely to be repressed as they admit dependency and the therapist covers up the wound.

The Return of the Repressed

CT is present in every analysis in the course of the fused living of therapist and patient. It cannot be avoided. The therapist's symptoms, defenses against unconscious feelings of CT, are, like the patient's, the obverse of the feeling itself, but contain a return of the repressed. Repressing sadistic anger, for instance, the therapist becomes silent, and like passive aggression, her silence inflicts pain even as it denies intentionality. As a result, it is the patient who is the overt hostile one. Self-observation picks up signals of a CT that places it for us. Analysis of our symptomatic act is a clue to use in self-awareness.

Is a CT experienced with all patients? What particular patient? In response to what partial aspect of the patient? Has a CT appeared early or late in treatment? What is the nature at that time of the patient's transference? Is a CT a sudden emergency defense reaction to a breakthrough of affect by the patient? Is there a persistent pressure from the patient that is beginning to overwhelm the therapist so that "once and for all" the therapist will now forbid it?

Boredom and sleepiness are often the therapist's way of blocking her erotic fantasies about a patient. Sometimes sleepiness is an expression of deprivation feelings in relation to the patient's resistance and reflects the therapist's earlier dependent "oral" need. Perhaps the therapist finds herself daydreaming about observations on life to make to the patient as the hour continues. This is a signal of CT. Are the therapist and patient in competition?

A training analyst (Cohen 1952) made note of some sixteen tangible signals of CT taken from her own work and consultations with others. The following are her formulations with some omissions.

1. The therapist has an unreasoning dislike for the patient.

2. The therapist cannot identify with the patient, who seems unreal or mechanical. The therapist feels no emotional response.

3. The therapist becomes overemotional in regard to the patient's troubles.

4. The therapist likes the patient excessively.

5. The therapist dreads the hours with a particular patient or is uncomfortable during them.

6. The therapist is preoccupied with the patient to an unusual degree in intervals between hours.

7. The therapist goes to sleep during hours, becomes very drowsy, or is preoccupied with personal affairs.

8. The therapist is habitually late with a particular patient or shows other disturbance in the time arrangement, such as always running over at the end of the hour.

9. The therapist gets into arguments with the patient.

10. The therapist exhibits unusual vulnerability to the patient's criticism.

11. The patient seems to consistently misunderstand the therapist's interpretations or never agrees with them. The therapist never considers that the interpretations actually may be wrong.

12. The therapist tries to elicit affect from the patient—for instance, by provocative or dramatic statements.

13. The therapist is overconcerned about the confidentiality of his or her work with the patient.

14. The therapist is angrily sympathetic with the patient regarding his mistreatment by some authority figure.

15. The therapist feels impelled to do something active in respect to the patient.

16. The patient appears in the therapist's dreams.

Once CT is perceived, self-analysis or consultation with a colleague can make it understood. The experience may temporarily undermine confidence or even increase an opposite tendency, but it usually leads the therapist to greater effectiveness.

Identity Crisis

CT reactions cannot be reduced to a few infantile traumas. Cultural change itself brings CT reaction. The therapist has mitigated her childhood reaction of shock and superego anxiety, and become relativistic and broadminded. For example, premarital sex or common use of "dirty" words that her parents interdicted no longer cause her anxiety. Now new shocking issues emerge, like frank statements of women's lust. New "dirty" words represent physical reality and new social liberation. The therapist's rigidity makes her feel she is reactionary. Since the therapist self-image is one of sophistication and tolerance, she proceeds to rationalize. Defenses of her CT can make her blind to cultural change and take the form of focusing on the patient's exhibitionism, the patient's low self-image, the patient's defense against closeness, the patient's aggression to the therapist.

If the therapist is willing to admit to her shocked reaction, the patient often helps her out with the signs of changing times. "Are you kidding? It does suck! Come on, doc!" Knowing he is human, the patient knows the therapist is human, too, and both must accept the fact of changing mores. This interchange is nonanalytic, but it is not antianalytic. In the therapeutic alliance, the therapist and patient can weather many storms.

Sometimes a therapist is so engaged in new enterprise, or is so focused on some insight, that a CT breaks through only to be understood and felt as humorous as quickly as a slip of the tongue.

A young male analyst, in his first supervision, had finally been able to suggest to his patient "try the couch." He consciously had felt this as difficult, as it presented him, the therapist, as "a real analyst." After a silence from the couch obeying the injunction to say whatever came to mind, to the therapist's astonishment, he heard his patient saying "I feel as if you were going to knife me in the back." "Sit up!" the therapist said. "Look at me. Do I look as if I would knife you? I'm here to help you!" Far from feeling him as a usurper and child his patient in the transference experienced him as a dangerous assassin. The therapist was caught out, unaware and unanalytic.

A patient may have a problem that seems "natural" to the therapist. It is ego-syntonic. For instance, the patient may suffer anxiety over confessing that she needs to urinate or feels some body stirring. The superego anxiety that the patient experiences is *this time* identical with the therapist's. When the patient begins to work on her inhibitions and sense of shame, she receives only reassurance from the therapist. "Why are you so self-critical?" asks the therapist. "Doesn't everybody have such feelings?" Encountering the problem might gain both therapist and patient another degree of freedom.

Vested Interests

We have talked of narcissistic CT needs; of unresolved conflicts, patient anxiety and libidinal striving; and of a sense of identity welded to important and unimportant adaptations. We are now ready to consider a CT that reflects the therapist's specific emotional investment in the therapist's character. The role of the therapist is surely a role of the inner self of the therapist. At the deep level of sublimation of instinctual aggressive and libidinal needs, the private and professional person are one dynamic system. We must therefore take into account that the mastery of trauma and permanent neurotic disturbances is integral in character, and that the therapist's character will be under fire in the conduction of therapy.

When an important sublimation in the therapist's character is threatened, an urgent sudden acute CT may develop. Self-awareness of the points of origin of the therapist's motivations in being a therapist then come under consideration. Usually the therapist is operating at a mature level in respect to "deinstinctualization," and sublimation. That is to say, infantile fixations merge with other, more mature needs. For instance, the pleasures of easy access to mother, of looking without being seen, of feeding, of introjecting, have truly merged with other, more mature needs and have found "higher," "sublimated" expressions in learning, observing, nurturing, and comprehending. Again, the need to inflict pain is sublimated and has emerged as the ability to "hate within limits" and the ability to set limits in turn.

It is very unpleasant to have the original infantile feelings threaten important sublimations when aroused "by the patient." When the threatening arousal is repressed, it forms a troublesome CT. The therapist who cannot handle such a CT may act it out.

For example, unable to resist an avid curiosity and sublimate the need to know the secrets, a therapist angrily exclaimed "bull-shit!" when the patient denied sexual feelings. We name the therapist's hostile response "acting out" because within the therapist there is a memory of infantile helpless frustration that the therapist is "acting out" rather than remembering. The therapist is not acting—that is, making believe—he is avidly curious and angry, although she may excuse his behavior as one of therapeutic intent. With such behavior the therapist has once more tried to solve his problem by the same hostile behavior that failed to solve it in the past. Awareness of such CT sets new adaptive measures in motion. Often consultation about the difficulty is particularly useful because the unconscious is so available and motivation is on hand.

Why choose a field like psychotherapy, one of such depriving incognito and altruistic concern with the liberation and actualization of another besides the self? The therapist may be doing to others as she would like to be done by, and experiencing mature satisfaction in living up to an ego ideal, as well as satisfaction in earning a living and professional pride.

The Human Condition

Another CT experience of trauma, more readily accessible to awareness and more easily partialized and mastered, is identification of the therapist's "private grief" with some tragedy of the patient's. For example, when I began training as an analyst, my personal analysis had been completed. I can remember thinking that no one had told me that as I worked I would reenter personal trauma again and again, and master it again and again; that as an analyst, as I expressed it, my analysis would go on and on. This was in reference to dealing with the death of my patient's father. My own father's death, a trauma in my adult life, had been the precipitating cause of my own analysis and our relationship a central theme. The CT response was quite available to me. It was a kind of feeling of "no, no, no, not again!" The working through, of course, proved to be rewarding.

Grief, helpless illness, costly separation, can temporarily threaten the therapist's innate love of life, that is, her "primary narcissism." Closeness to the tragedy of the human condition is hard; flight from such closeness in defense of CT is not an option for a therapist. Depressive mood swings might be an indication that being a therapist involves too much personal risk and a more defended role in life might be considered.

CT, an Effective Agent of Therapy

Many of the considerations we have reviewed must seem to the reader to echo the mother who requested her husband to go down to the basement and "see what the children are doing and tell them to stop!" Rather, as the science of psychoanalytic therapy evolves, recognition increases that CT, when recognized, is an effective, indispensable tool in treatment. It is the first step of empathy, upon which intuition depends; it is the foundation of insight into patient transference, and it is the source of engaged participative and affective psychoanalytic therapy.

As a male therapist listens to a patient, he hears how anxious the young man is over his new title and promotion at work. Somewhere, the therapist identifies with the feeling. He himself is anxious in the same way over his entrance into an advanced academic institution. He feels "for the patient" and, for a moment, "as the patient." He does not lose himself in this CT nor defend against it; he "recovers himself." He recognizes the patient's feeling as a fear of exhibitionism and phallic competition with the patient's show-off father. From the fluctuating interplay, the therapist can predict that the patient will gain insight if he reminds him of how much even as a teenager the patient had lived in the shadow of his father. The therapist speaks empathetically of the patient's shyness at that time, and then encourages the patient to speak of his new position and even role-play himself in the new role. (Shafer 1959)

CT as a guide to hidden implications of transference must be experienced to be understood. The therapist feels almost as if she were in a play and a part had been assigned to her by the patient-director. She experiences herself feeling and acting according to the patient's script. The patient assigns a part to the therapist as he engages in an unconscious compulsion to repeat with the therapist the significant experiences of his past life, and to recreate in the therapist the significant figures of his past. The CT experience of being placed in this role is "read" by the therapist and provides a map to the patient. For example:

A patient refused to talk. (Her shut lips repeated hidden memories of a stage of near anorexic refusal to eat in her early childhood.) As the female therapist related to this refusal, session after session, she was led, step by step, to "feel," in a CT like an inadequate, desperate mother. The therapist began to hold back, controlling her growing panic by passive withdrawal. The patient, then, finally, tearfully, began to speak. She accused the therapist of not wanting her for a patient, of feeling burdened and rejecting, of not having anything left to give her patient. Now the therapist understood. She had just been forced into playing the ambivalent guilty mother and then into acting out the mother's projection of her own inadequacy onto the child. The therapist suggested to the patient that this may have been her perception of her mother as a little girl. The patient "remembered" how she would sit for sad hours, skinny and stubborn, refusing to swallow. She remembered she was a "very bad eater" and a very bad girl. She remembered that her poor mother had tried every way she could to get her to eat. "You felt your mother blamed you and did not want such a difficult child as a daughter." The therapist had received the message of the transference in a CT and now projected it back to the patient, and now the patient could cry and she, too, could read herself. The therapist then called the patient's attention to how well she did relate the story.

In both instances, the one of the empathy and the one of the therapist's insight into her patient's transference perception of mother, the patients had "a corrective emotional experience" from the affectual response of the therapist (French and Alexander 1946). The first patient experienced a father figure who did wish him to show his feelings and, in the session, take center stage. The second patient discovered that with a "mother" who could provide good food (that is, empathy), she could be a good girl and eat (that is, talk and remember). Had the man therapist not controlled a display of his own feelings, he would have taken stage himself with a reassuring story of his own difficulty. Had the woman therapist "proved" how resistant her patient was and recounted her many efforts to help, she too would have projected the inadequacy she had introjected and repeated a pathogenic parent's reaction. Such interchanges in analysis have been called "a unique way of arranging for the common place—the common place of experimentation and learning through human intercourse what has been lost to the patient." (Berman 1949) As active participants, through CT, the two therapists supplied the affect that allowed genuine interaction.

Dedication

The therapist's resonance to the patient resembles the interaction between a mother and her infant. Dedication to the patient's welfare is an attribute of an effective analyst. During the dedicated early years of psychoanalytically oriented therapeutic work, the young therapist often gets remarkable results (Berman 1949).

Immersed in the experience of the process the therapist rarely verbalizes dedicated feelings. Through kindly acceptance, patience, and emotional engagement, the patient intuitively feels the therapist's dedication. Sometimes the patient is directly aware of those feelings. Often both therapist and patient count on an alliance and trust that underlies many stormy sessions or resistances.

A patient of mine, a college student, had been sullen and tearful for a number of sessions, reliving the years of his early life when his father and mother's bitter quarrels over money destroyed the family. Now, the last session of the month, he came late, and at the end of the session jumped up, and red in the face, stamped over to my desk. He threw a bunch of $1 bills prepared in his pocket over desk and floor. "There you are. All you want is your money!" he shouted. Taken by surprise, my reaction was a flood of empathy. "You know better than that," I said mildly and kindly. The patient turned and gave me a smile of joy and relief. "See you Monday," he said. And we both laughed.

Dedication cannot always protect the therapist from CT or poor impulse control. The helpful rules of the game, the ethics of the profession, are usually supported in terms of guarding the patient's transference experience. For instance, the analyst must not accept significant gifts from patients, so that the patient may not be permitted defensive acting out. Perhaps the therapist's formulation that the rules are for protection of the patient is itself a CT. Perhaps therapists do not want to admit that dedication to the patient is limited and that therapists must be protected from greed, like other humans, by authoritative ethical injunctions, be it from tradition or the threat of official group action.

Patients are in a very vulnerable position in respect to therapists. A therapist needs strength to withstand the temptations of exploiting her influence. A therapist at times needs a conscience, a superego, that firmly and permanently commands "hands off!" forbidden fruit. If not in control, she should seek help long before the unethical impulse is acted upon. When therapists abuse their role and take physical advantage of patients for sexual gratification, they are helplessly giving in to an infantile, erotic impulse that has been invoked by intimate proximity and a position of power. Not only group pressure, but realistic acceptance of human weakness urges submission to ethical standards. The rules are there for the therapist's protection as well as the patient's.

The Humanness of the Analyst

Psychoanalytically oriented therapists feel strange about revealing how they actually analyze in the office. This embarrassment comes from respect for confidentiality, but also from awareness of the humanness of their behavior and experience in the office, in contrast to traditional theoretical models. Actually, the experienced therapist knows that the role of the therapist is a role of the self, that CT has been in the background for the therapist from the beginning. However, even the experienced therapist feels ashamed when she is out of the office to "admit" her office humanness. The humanness of the therapist (Fenichel 1941) was clearly present in Freud's office and has been true since, with less or more open admission. Humanness is only slowly being claimed theoretically as an integral part of psychoanalytic work. Psychoanalytic theory officially accepted the therapist-patient alliance partly in response to humanist impact, partly from the growing psychoanalytic focus on ego psychology, and partly from the English school's exploration of the social growth of the infant, formulated in object relationship terms. Yet the therapist qua therapist, theoretically, was to be a cold surgeon, a bland screen, operating through the transference "on the patient's psychic tissues." But in the alliance he now could and should be a warm, human, friendly person (Greenson 1968).

Freud (1915) granted that the patient did receive "a certain amount of transference gratification." Fenichel (1941) allowed the therapist humanness; treatment was not to be isolated from life, and "the patient should always be able to rely upon the humanness of the analyst." The question, then, was reformulated, no longer one of blank screen versus human gratification but one of object need for the patient—"how much and what kind of satisfaction is needed?" (Balint 1950) For the therapist, how much giving, how much staying outside? Hopefully the therapist is a "person whose dynamics provoke constructive interpsychic changes within the patient." (Whitaker and Malone 1953)

Nonetheless, only some of the therapist's reactions will be appropriate at any given time for an optimal emotional climate and an opportunity for patient-object relationship experience. The timing, like the transference, is determined by the patient. In a sense, the art of response and control of a CT is greater as the human factor is found to be so strong a dynamic. For example, when the therapist shares an adolescent's wonderfully new and cherished ability to "intellectualize," and deep "beautiful" talk ensues, the therapist must nonetheless tactfully and determinedly give priority to reflection, acceptance, and mastery of feelings (Meeks 1975).

Allowed to be human, the therapist finds she is more relaxed, engaged, and empathetic. Affect is greater and, with less repression, there is more flexibility, variety, and expressiveness. The therapist enjoys her work more. To do so safely she also needs to be more secure, clear, and firm in relationship to process and CT. The patient is there to learn his own unconscious, not that of the therapist. Insight into her own unconscious is a royal road to the patient's unconscious. The patient's transference must be read, implemented, and responded to from the therapist's CT, but the CT must be perceived, understood, and managed by the therapist. It is the therapist who is responsible for mastery of the signals and causes of CT.

To some therapists the openness of being human creates an anxious CT of its own. The comfort of being incognito that may have brought the private self to the profession of therapy seems threatened. This CT must be understood, but also it is of help to remember that like "good enough mothering," "good enough relating" is well within normal friendliness. With new, positive acceptance of CT feelings instead of denial (new positive cathexis of CT), CT becomes less repressed, seeking expression and tempting the therapist to disclose it.

Disclosure of CT

Observation of CT by the therapist for self-analysis, reading of CT for insight and empathy in work with a patient, sharing of human affect with a patient all call for considerable insight and art. Disclosure of CT to the patient is of a different order of interference with the delicate balance of interpersonal and transference responses.

There is new and fairly general agreement that in the interest of trust and "reality testing," a CT response by the therapist should be admitted when the patient overtly chooses to react to it or when it has clearly, if covertly, entered the transference.

Disclosure of CT to the patient is now in debate. Even those who feel that it is an important dramatic tool for inducing the patient to encounter his own transference (Little 1951) warn that they advise the therapist to "admit" to CT, "not confess it," a justified concern. The patient, they believe, is unconsciously aware, in any case, of the therapist's CT, and thus disclosure is part of analysis. For example, if a therapist were to say, "That's a terrible thing you did to your friend. If a friend of mine acted like that I would never speak to her again," the explanation would be that the patient, in confessing his cruel behavior, already knew and meant the therapist to disapprove because he wanted help with change, and because he hated himself for such behavior.

More conservative review of CT disclosure suggests that its emotional impact on a patient and the emotional catharsis for the therapist charges the atmosphere of therapy intrusively. The therapist's "patient vector," her CT, may seriously limit the patient's options. Perhaps the disclosure of CT is itself a CT need that the therapist has not handled. Nonetheless, as analytic therapy focuses on affectual object relationships and developmental lacks, disclosure of the therapist's CT may prove in the future to be a vital factor in the patient's growth.

Ted Saretsky

The Middle Phase of Treatment

The process of psychoanalytic psychotherapy does not follow a straight path to insight and rehabilitation. Instead, it is more like putting together, a few pieces at a time, an immense and enormously complicated jigsaw puzzle (with some of the pieces missing). Change is significantly more dependent on patient readiness than on the accuracy of analytic interpretations. If the work proceeds too rapidly and the therapist precipitously attempts to cajole, suggest, direct, or pressure the patient to make healthier decisions, there is the strong possibility that the treatment situation itself will become traumatic. Under these circumstances, patients frequently become more guarded, defensive, and agitated. If these resistances become strong enough they can create discouragement, long stalemates, and premature terminations.

In order to counteract these negative reactions, the initial phase of therapy focuses on establishing an effective working alliance between doctor and patient. The patient's contribution to a positive relationship stems from a wish to overcome her illness, her sense of helplessness, her conscious and rational willingness to cooperate, and her ability to follow the therapist's interpretations. Those traits in the therapist that persuade the patient of the doctor's good intentions, compassion, and expertness include his being natural, straightforward, respectful, and understanding. Over a period of time, a good working climate hopefully develops that lends itself to openness, mutuality of interests, and collaboration.

The establishment and maintenance of a durable, reliable working relationship constitutes the opening phase of psychoanalytic psychotherapy. The next phase of treatment, called the middle phase, is usually considered the heart of the therapeutic process. It is the longest period of therapeutic work and extends until both parties seriously discuss termination. The bulk of this time is devoted to exploring, analyzing, working through, and resolving the patient's symptoms and emotional and characterological problems.

Since everyone's background, life experiences, and personality differ, there are an infinite variety of problems that can emerge during the middle phase. Freud liked to use the analogy of a chess game, with the opening, middle, and termination phases of analysis paralleling the opening, middle, and end games of chess. Freud felt that only the opening and end phases of analysis had definite technical rules and a predictable course. In both chess and analysis, the protagonists must find their own way during the middle phase.

Perhaps the best way to systematically understand the many complex phenomena operating during this phase is to discuss the various technical tools and psychological concepts at the therapist's disposal, and then later in the chapter to carefully examine how these can be applied to emerging treatment problems.

Interpretation

The chief technical tool at the therapist's command in approaching the analytic task is interpretation. The source of interpretive statements is the therapist's inner assessment of the patient's personality makeup, the patient's presentation of problems and the causative factors in his past that have contributed to current difficulties. *Clinical interpretation* is defined here as a statement (or a set of related statements) to the patient that points to, names, and sometimes causally accounts for the patient's present most prepotent unrecognized behavior. Only on the basis of first understanding what's going on in the patient can the therapist know what to interpret and how and when to do so. The guiding principle in timing interpretations, relative to the whole of treatment and to individual sessions, is that of readiness. This boils down to the question: Is the patient's awareness close enough to consciousness that therapeutic interventions will set the stage for a collaborative dialogue? The therapist uses the patient's reactions as a gauge for determining readiness.

Freud's original statements regarding interpretation focused on making the unconscious conscious, thereby revealing hidden meanings. More precise contemporary definitions of interpretation would encompass naming, identifying, categorizing, denoting, describing, specifying, labeling, or translating the patient's associations.

Some illustrations might be helpful at this point.

Karen had a very unsettling childhood that made her constantly strive for love and security by trying hard to please. She was aware of how resentful she was at having to make such an effort and offered this as an explanation for why she was unmotivated and unsuccessful in establishing relationships. Karen was convinced that unless she did what others wanted, she would be rejected. The therapist gradually brought out her own rejecting attitudes, the fact that now not only was she rebelling against trying too hard, but she wasn't trying at all. Karen was being rejected in her current life not because she wasn't trying to please but because she was cold, indifferent, and hostile. Further discussions led to interpretations such as: "Now your sense of entitlement is so exaggerated that you act as though the men owe you something without deserving anything back from you."

A mother had come for consultation regarding her six-year-old daughter, who was described as negativistic, rebellious, and unhappy. The mother reported an incident where a man in the supermarket offered the child a pear and tried to chat in a friendly way with her. The daughter shied away and didn't respond to his overtures. Upon leaving the mother screamed at her daughter to learn to be friendly, to speak up, to stop being so selfish. During the same session, the mother told of how good she felt this past week when she disagreed with her husband and, for once, didn't worry about his temper. The therapist wondered aloud whether there could be any connection between the woman's lifelong struggle to learn to be more independent and not appease and her condemnation of her daughter for daring not to be so nice.

In the first illustration, Karen was made aware of something she did not see; namely, irrational, ultimately self-defeating demands that she placed on others. In the second example, the mother was encouraged to explore her overidentification with the daughter, with the further possibility that the daughter might be acting out some of the mother's underlying resentment. In both instances, the therapist allies himself with the healthy, progressive part of the patient's ego (for example, the wish for close relationships; the wish to be independent; the wish to not have to seek approval). In so doing, the therapist's interpretations are designed to gradually undermine the threatening, accusing, punishing self-concept that almost all patients have.

Resistance

If all that was necessary for patient progress was the achievement and transmission of intellectual insight, then psychotherapy would simply require intelligence and cooperation on the part of the patient and therapist. It would take a short while to clarify and agree upon the core problem, the historical roots would not take very long to track down, recommendations could be made to change maladaptive behavior patterns, symptoms would be alleviated, and treatment could be terminated in a period of months. In actual practice, we discover that habits are not so easy to break, that patients have strong, unconscious investments in not changing even though they are in pain, and that guilt and anxiety are very influential in perpetuating self-destructive behavior even when the patient is highly motivated. The therapist has to continuously contend with obstacles the patient creates that tend to impede progress.

These obstacles, which Freud (1912a) labeled "resistance," are more thoroughly discussed in Chapter 4. In this section I'd like to concentrate on specific patterns of resistance that are most likely to occur during the middle phase of treatment.

A patient had been seen for six months regarding a mutually destructive marriage whereby her husband was insensitive, uncaring, and emotionally detached. In the midst of building up the courage to separate from this man, the patient went into a severe depression, developed multiple somatic complaints, became very insecure, and began to lose confidence in her decision. These symptoms were identified as resistance, and were interpreted in terms of the patient's fear of independence and anxiety over separating herself from a love object. By reverting to a clinging, dependent role, she succeeded in obscuring her dread of loneliness in being on her own and the guilt that she felt about hurting her husband.

Another patient had a background of cruel, unloving parents who made him feel they were doing him a favor by tolerating him. As treatment progressed, the patient developed greater feelings of trust, openness, and acceptance of his need for others than ever before. This growth spurt was suddenly interrupted by the intrusion of paranoid thoughts, suspiciousness, and hostility directed primarily toward the therapist. As the patient turned to others more, his conscience told him that he should be grateful, indebted, and eternally appreciative. This guilt made him resent what he was getting because he then felt in the power of others, under their control. The hostility was interpreted as a tension-reducing device, a way of regaining his own autonomy at the cost of a lack of intimacy and a cold, barren life.

The extent to which it is necessary to focus on the analysis of resistance illustrates the difference between intensive psychotherapy and a counseling orientation. Psychological counseling is characterized by terms such as supportive, situational, educational, problem solving, conscious awareness, emphasis on normals, and short term. Psychotherapy is defined as a more inclusive reeducation of the individual at both the conscious and unconscious levels. The basic aims of psychotherapy are to assist the client to gain perceptual reorganization, to integrate the consequent insights into her personality structure, and to work out methods of handling feelings originating deep within her personality. Her existing defenses are usually modified to such a degree that readjustment is obtained. Thus psychotherapy emphasizes depth of involvement in the personality and is more concerned with alleviating pathological conditions, whereas counseling is not so deep. Counseling also stresses more rational planning, problem solving, and support for situational pressures arising in the everyday lives of normal people.

In general, psychological counselors see resistance as something that opposes progress and problem solving and therefore is something that should be reduced as much as possible. The therapist, in contrast, sees resistance as an important phenomenon for intensive analysis. If he can understand the patient's unique form of resistance, he will more likely be able to help her understand and change her personality. The aim of psychotherapy, therefore, is not just to "find out the patient's secret." Rather, it is to discover how the patient hides the secret.

There are innumerable forms of resistance, but it might be help-ful to indicate some of the subtler as well as more glaring examples. For example, the patient forgets her appointment; comes late; fre-quently cancels appointments; is always complaining that she isn't being helped; frequently criticizes the therapist; fails to listen care-fully or understand what's being told to her; comes in high; remains silent; engages in intellectual discussions using sophisticated psy-chological terminology; desires to terminate prematurely; doesn't bring in material that's relevant, important, and meaningful; makes unreasonable demands on the therapist; or is consistently skeptical about interpretations.

The patient's resistance can also take less aggressive forms, as, for example, always trying to please the therapist; agreeing un-equivocally with everything he says; refusing to get emotionally involved; becoming unnecessarily dependent on the therapist; being facetious; talking abstractly or philosophically; seeing the problem as existing outside of herself; constantly qualifying everything she says, or inhibiting expressions of hostility, anxiety, or guilt.

Interpretive statements intended to consistently confront the pa-tient with the ongoing nature of her resistance represent the heart of the middle phase of treatment.

Transference

Transference is another concept central to psychoanalytic tech-nique, and is elaborated on in Chapter 3. In terms of the middle phase of treatment, let me offer several illustrations that highlight the emergence of transference phenomena as treatment progresses.

Jack's mother was extremely self-sacrificing and devoted. She worked and taxed the family budget to the maximum to send him to an out-of-town college, rarely left him alone on Saturday night to go out with her husband, and was consistently doting and complimentary. In his early twenties, Jack's relationship with women was volatile, sadistic, and withholding. He viewed females as grasping, manipulative, and dependent. His reaction to his female analyst was markedly ambivalent. He was forever rebelling and then making guilty restitutions. During one session in particular, Jack apologized if he inconvenienced the therapist by changing the appointment time. When the therapist questioned what prompted this unnecessary nicety, Jack had the following association: "I feel guilty for having put you out. You might resent my doing this. I want you to like me. You might not be interested in me if you're irritated." Further exploration of similar instances of ingratiating behavior (for example, "I'm not sure whether this is what you wanted me to say") reveals Jack's deep resentment toward the supposed sacrifices that others were making on his behalf. The conscious part of him felt appreciative; unconsciously, he felt obligated, controlled, and angry.

The significance of transference in this case was that the patient's behavior with the therapist was a replication of an earlier pattern of behavior with the mother. The therapist can use this information to better understand early dependency dynamics, offer the patient new options for behavior with an authority figure, and clarify puzzling ambivalences in existing peer relationships on the outside.

Rhonda's parents were very good to her in a materialistic way. She came to feel that in exchange for this goodness, she wasn't supposed to feel disappointed or cheated. When these feelings arose in the form of jealousy, hurt, or anger, she tended to feel selfish and guilty. After six months of treatment, she revealed that she frequently didn't let the therapist know that she didn't understand her. Her explanation was that she didn't want to sound stupid. The analyst asked her if she was afraid that he would feel stupid if she said she didn't understand him. Subsequent discussion indicated that in her relationship with her parents, Rhonda came to feel that if openly expressed, her dissatisfaction would hurt their feelings, make them feel that she was ungrateful, and cause them to reject her.

Here, the therapist employed the patient's reactions toward him to assist her in realizing that she was misidentifying the therapist. By projecting onto him attitudes that the parents might have had, she was wrongly anticipating his reactions and thereby becoming unnecessarily defensive. This interpretation encouraged the patient to start examining other relationships where she kept herself aloof, secretive, and superficial.

Working Through

In his paper "Remembering, Repeating and Working Through" (1914c), Freud introduced the concept of *repetition compulsion*, which he described as the patient's tendency to repeat a past experience and action instead of remembering. This habit is unconscious, is particularly tenacious, and requires constant clarification until the patient understands what the therapist is talking about. Freud suggested that it is necessary to do more than simply tell the patient that she is resisting or name the resistance. In order to overcome it, the patient needs time to get to know the resistance better and to discover the repressed feelings that feed it. Freud coined the phrase *working through* to describe the process of constantly going back to the raw data of the session and trying to glean new understandings and fresh perspectives. Freud didn't give much credence to the "aha experience"—the illuminating revelation, the sudden miraculous understanding. He believed that "this working through of the resistance may in practice turn out to be an arduous task for the subject of the analysis and a trial of patience for the analyst. Nevertheless, it is a part of the work which effects the greatest changes in the patient and which distinguishes analytic treatment from any kind of treatment by suggestion." (1914b, pp. 155–156)

The same emphasis on repetition as the dynamic force in learning can be found in the writings of an early student of Freud—Otto Fenichel. "Systematic and consistent interpretive work, both within and without the framework of transference, can be described as educating the patient to produce continually less distorted derivatives until his fundamental, instinctual conflicts are recognizable." Of course, this is not a single operation resulting in a single act of abreaction: it is, rather, a chronic process of working through, which shows the patient again and again the same conflicts and her usual way of reacting to them, but from new angles and new connections (1945, p. 31). In a similar vein, Freida Fromm Reichmann, a more contemporary psychoanalyst, has stated, "any understanding, any new piece of awareness which has been gained by interpretive clarification, has to be reconquered and tested time and again in new connections and contacts with other interlocking experiences, which may or may not have to be subsequently approached interpretively in their own right. That is the process to which psychoanalysts refer when speaking of the necessity of repeatedly 'working through.' " (1950, p. 141)

The reason that effective psychotherapy generally takes place over a long period of time is that a single abreactive experience is insufficient for the ego to gain mastery over material it has to keep in repression for so many years. It is not easy to break off habits even if we know that they are not good for us. Once an important trend or pattern is identified, the therapist has to persistently attempt to explore it in all its ramifications and in as elaborate detail as possible. The relationship of the trend (for example, dependency, withdrawal from pain, fear of abandonment) to other aspects of the psychic life, and an investigation of the conflicts it engenders, must be examined by drawing the patient's attention to and eliciting associations to every trend manifestation. The analyst goes about doing this in an orderly, sequential way. First, he attempts to arouse the patient's curiosity and interest in a particular piece of defensive behavior. Next the patient is encouraged to discover that she plays a prominent part in her behavior, that she is actively bringing about the very thing that is disburbing her (such as rejection, disappointment, or loneliness). The therapist's next task is to patiently introduce the patient to the possibility that the defense has a purpose and that the purpose is probably to avoid experiencing some kind of anxiety or threat. The patient learns that what is avoided and how it is avoided are both historically determined. In this way, the patient is gradually led to sort out past from present, the confusion of which is the core of most neuroses.

When this sequence of interpretations is repeated often enough, the patient begins to integrate and accept parts of herself that she was previously embarrassed by or felt guilty about—for example, you're not necessarily bad if you hurt somebody else's feelings; giving priority to your own feelings is not selfish; enjoying sex is not sinful; feeling angry and expressing it can be constructive and does not have to jeopardize close relationships; you do not have to be what other people expect of you in order to be loved by them, and so on. By consciously examining core conflicts from many different angles, with appropriate feelings emerging and receiving acknowledgment and acceptance, the patient's ego gains access to split-off parts of herself that were heretofore treated as bad and kept out of awareness.

This is not as simple as it might sound, however. Just when the patient seems to be understanding herself better, she starts resisting again and acts as though she cannot remember what she readily accepted only last session. The interpretive process must begin all over again. The therapist has to find a new occasion or a different way of making his interpretations clear. Dream analysis may be helpful in this regard. Or, the patient may report a revealing incident that she does not consciously recognize as being related to what is being resisted. The therapist runs through the interpretive cycle again, hoping that the patient can grasp the connection between the current conflict and previously discussed conflict situations. Ego building is slowly taking place. Each time, the patient's capacity to learn from the past is accelerated. As in the analysis of transference, the patient has to be confronted over and over again with all possible variations of warded-off material and her entire repertoire of techniques for warding off. The therapeutic task is not complete until unconscious conflictual complexes are detoxified, become significantly less threatening to the ego, and are replaced by more adaptive modes of behavior.

Therapy is near termination when the patient has clarified and accepted her present emotional difficulties, rationally understands the historical roots of her problems and feelings, and integrates these awarenesses in terms of the complex relationship between past and present events and in terms of the relationship between herself and the therapist (transference). Successfully treated patients report the following types of changes in themselves:

1. A deeper grasp of the meaning of their presenting symptoms, the functions that they serve, the hidden gains in remaining neurotic

2. A more dynamic insight into the ways that the environment affects them and they affect the environment

3. More positive feelings about self and others

4. Reduced defensiveness and greater awareness of when one is being defensive

However, all the intellectual insight in the world is virtually worthless unless the individual is simultaneously experimenting with trying out her new behavior. Everyday experience with real-life people, satisfying conversation, healthy self-assertion, pleasurable sexual encounters, the cultivation of a good friendship, and success at work offer continuous positive reinforcement that encourages new integrations and more mature behavior. The action stage in working through represents the proof of the pudding. In effect, as the patient describes her workaday dealings with others, she is indirectly informing the therapist of how much of the discussions have become incorporated and assimilated as a living part of herself. By so doing she alerts the therapist to what areas of her personality require further exploration.

Let us turn now to a case illustration that will demonstrate the mechanics of the working-through process.

Ronnie is a twenty-seven-year-old single woman who sought psychotherapy for episodes of depression, confusion, and recurrent anxiety attacks. Most of her presenting problems revolved around sadomasochistic relationships with men, where she was either excessively critical and aloof or she was taken for granted and abused.

The opening phase of treatment centered almost exclusively on her unsuccessful, bitter attempts to construct a positive relationship with men. Bit by bit, her early history unfolded, revealing a very traumatic childhood. Ronnie was raised in a tumultuous household consisting of two younger siblings whom she protected, a schizophrenic mother, and a weak, passive father. Ronnie's mother suffered a nervous breakdown when Ronnie was ten, and was hospitalized for three months when she was thirteen. For reasons of his own, the father could not bring himself to institutionalize the mother even though she was an extremely disruptive and destructive force at home. For example, the mother would act very strangely and erratically, insisting one day that everybody had to wear bathrobes over their clothes and eat only grapefruits for the main course; the next day she would change her mind and behave almost normally and forget her original demands. If Ronnie objected to these weird commands, the mother would go into an uncontrollable rage and the father would tell Ronnie not to provoke the mother, or otherwise he would leave. When they were alone, the father would use Ronnie as his confidante, his pillar of strength, and, in effect, made her his mother and a mother to the other children.

Much of the work that was accomplished during the first years of therapy was designed to reconstruct the impact of these genetic events into a meaningful, comprehensible pattern. The material then shifted to the possible connections between these historical experiences and Ronnie's current attitudes toward men and women. Little by little, Ronnie began to get in touch with the murderous rage that she felt toward her mother, father, sister, brother, and the men in her life for having to çater to their needs to the neglect of her own. Ronnie found the acceptance of this buried anger very difficult because of the guilt that it generated and the fear that expressing her negative feelings would lead to rejection and abandonment. If anything, her depression seemed to deepen during this time. Sometimes she would feel somewhat better for a while, then she would feel even worse.

I have presented the material and treatment progress of this case over a one-and-a-half-year period in a rather sketchy, condensed way, omitting many details of resistances, transferences, and the like. I simply want to set the stage for what follows: a critical session in Ronnie's course of treatment that I will use as a model of middle-phase therapeutic work.

Ronnie had been acting very negativistically toward the therapist for many weeks now. Her explanation was that she didn't feel free to talk about certain topics that interested her. She felt foolish, for example, bringing up experiences with men because invariably the emphasis would take the form of what she was doing wrong. In addition, Ronnie felt that the therapist would view her wish to get married and her resulting hurt and frustration at being single as not being a good enough reason for being in therapy.

At the beginning of this particular session, Ronnie strongly confronted the therapist with all of her pent-up anger. She was asked how she felt now that she let herself explode for the first time. "My anger toward you is all mixed up with the times I confronted my mother. Her reactions were always crazy. I had to read her moods constantly to see whether it was safe to disagree with her. I was always afraid she'd run out of the house and never come back. My father accused me of instigating her craziness if I stood up to her." The therapist asked Ronnie what she felt now that she had shown her anger toward him. "Funny, nervous. . .I don't know what to make of it. I keep imagining you wish I would get out of here and leave you alone, that maybe you wish you'd never started with me." The therapist asked her whether this is the way she really thinks he feels or "is it the way you're afraid I'm going to feel." At this point, Ronnie started sobbing uncontrollably. After a bit, she said, "You seem to be accepting my attack without kicking me out. I can't stand it—it's like you're too good to me." The therapist said, "There you go being self-sacrificing again." Ronnie said, "I'm afraid if I don't apologize, you'll be resentful. You won't like me." The therapist said, "You're hating yourself when you worry about my feelings too much and you project that resentment onto me." Ronnie answered, "Yes, I do resent having to worry about you all the time. Even while I was crying, I was concerned about what you were thinking." The therapist asked, "What did you think I was feeling?" Ronnie started crying again but this time it was a peaceful, gentle cry. "I was afraid you'd think that I was a drag; that I was imposing on you. I always wondered what it would be like to let myself go and not have to worry about the consequences." The therapist related the concern about "imposing" to her attitude with regard to sparing her already burdened parents. "The role that was most rewarded was to take responsibility for others and protect them from their weaknesses. Your mother and father were disappointments as parents but you spared them from realizing how much they failed."

Ronnie's response to this line of inquiry was as follows: "I never brought people to the house—I was ashamed as if it were my fault. I never realized before how angry I really must have been." Ronnie then went on to talk about her current relationships with men. "I'll do anything to keep them around. I won't disagree with them, I'll give in to them, I'll do what they want. Afterwards I'll get angry. Just like I've worked so hard for ten years to keep my family around. I'm tired of trying so hard; I'm mentally exhausted. I've spent too much of my time reading other people's minds to see how they feel and then acting accordingly. I feel too responsible for everybody."

Ronnie's background consisted of an eccentric, unpredictable, schizophrenic mother and a weak, inadequate, manipulative father. The mother's infantile demands combined with the father's need to indulge her by coercing Ronnie into denying her own sense of reality. The net effect was that Ronnie was put in an impossible bind. If she responded to the mother's outrageous behavior, the mother would become even more bizarre and the father would tyrannize Ronnie by threatening to leave. If she capitulated to this pressure by going along, she had to sacrifice the wish to have her own feelings considered. In effect, the immaturity of both parents prompted Ronnie to act out the role of being responsible for their feelings in order to gain acceptance. So that Ronnie could avoid abandonment and preserve her fragile sense of security, Ronnie's personality developed along masochistic lines. She began to hate her own ego in the name of the parents. Their suffering was greater; her reaction to her own hurt and happiness began to be experienced as selfish. For example, when Ronnie began to date as a teenager, the father was very critical and frequently reminded her that she was neglecting him. Even though Ronnie was attracted to boys, she lost interest in them until she left the house at age twenty-two. This self-sacrificing orientation was accompanied by another invidious trend. Ronnie accumulated an enormous amount of pent-up rage as a result of these appeasement maneuvers. Since the lessons of her childhood taught her that direct expression of this anger met with parental rejection and the threat of being orphaned, Ronnie learned to internalize and repress her oppositional feelings. This anger turned inward created the presenting clinical picture of depression, passivity, and helplessness.

The therapist's grasp of these dynamics made the recent upsurge of Ronnie's negative response to treatment comprehensible. Ronnie transferred onto the therapist a jealous, possessive father who resented her outside interests, particularly with men, and tried to manipulate her into the role of substituting for the wife he did not have. Consequently, Ronnie felt guilty about talking enthusiastically about new male acquaintances, tended to be overly critical of her interactions with them (to appease the therapist-father's jealousy), and then vented her hostility by attacking the therapist for her having to placate him. Ronnie's defensiveness regarding the wish to be married was explored in subsequent sessions. It was interpreted as her need to unnecessarily place what she imagined were the therapist's priorities before her own. Ronnie's resistance to therapy reflects the negative state of her ambivalence. Her underlying resentment at having to please is illustrated by her apathy, annoyance, and the explosive anger that intermittently revealed itself.

The therapist supported Ronnie's right to be angry. He helped her to understand that this represented her rebelliousness against having to be constantly defining herself in terms of what other people expected of her. The therapist identified the oppositional trend as part of her autonomy, self-assertion, and independence. He tried to help Ronnie to see that her insecurity cut down on the range of options that she allowed herself—rebellion, appeasement, or withdrawal. It was suggested that perhaps Ronnie's bad luck with men followed a similar pattern. She put so much pressure on herself to be what they wanted her to be that she ultimately felt exploited and resentful. Her emotional conflicts became even more glaring if she really liked a man. This would intensify her wish to please him to the extent that she felt as though she were losing her own identity and becoming completely subordinate to the man's needs. The anxiety that this engendered made her choose men who abused her, because then she could feel freer because she didn't care as much. Over the next few months, Ronnie slowly began to see that the resistance to the therapist at this juncture in treatment was a function of her gratitude and strong dependency upon him. Ronnie felt appreciative of the therapist's help, but instead of accepting this as her right, she felt obligated to repay him. The form this restitution took was gradually seen as similar to the payments that she had to offer to the mother and father—denial of her individuality.

Over a period of time following this session, Ronnie allowed herself to behave more like a peer with the therapist. More importantly, she began to take personal responsibility during the sessions for what topics were to be given priority and focused upon. She allowed herself to disagree with the therapist without being terrified that he would reject her. She became noticeably less prone to make the therapist her judge and jury. Simultaneously, she began to become more experimental and adventurous in relations with men. She behaved more independently, becoming more discriminating and extroverted. She stopped pressuring herself to get them to like her and so she started feeling more at ease with them.

This process of obtaining more and more insight and personality change through repeated and varied examination of conflicts and problems constitutes the essence of the middle stage of treatment. Interactions between free associations, resistances, interpretations, the emergence of transferences, and working through are the central ingredients the therapist has to work with.

Dream Interpretation

Most therapists who operate from a psychoanalytic framework find the exploration of dreams and fantasies indispensable. Each dream has significance in that it embodies a current concern of the patient within the context of a characteristic style that she has of interpreting her own experiences. The hidden meaning of dreams can embrace long-forgotten memories; secret thoughts toward parents and siblings; current attitudes, impulses, feelings, and defenses against them; representations of different aspects of the self (for example, the real me versus the me I think I should be); and attitudes toward the therapist.

A month after the session when Ronnie was starting to feel better and become more social, she dreamed that she was having a good time at a party but that her mother was sitting in the corner dressed in rags. Ronnie came to the session somewhat down and could not understand why, since her real life was taking a turn for the better. She got in touch with the fact that in the midst of enjoying herself, her mind flitted to her mother's wasted life. "I find it hard to get it through my head that she's a separate person, that she had her chance, now let me have mine." The therapist suggested that previously she had inhibited her positive feelings to a stifling degree; now, at least, she allowed herself to have nice experiences first and then felt somewhat guilty. "They can't take that away from you." Ronnie then went on to describe some of the ambivalence she felt in the past week in terms of spending more money on herself. She bought some expensive clothes and made plans for an ambitious European vacation with a friend. "It's not my fault that my mother's sitting in that corner. I'm making myself do right by me. I still feel strange—it doesn't seem like me being so good to myself. . . ."

The middle phase of treatment involves using every manifestation of the patient's conflicts regarding her separation from the mother (and/or other significant figures) as grist for the therapeutic mill. Dreams are useful as a diagnostic indication of (1) how successfully the patient is accomplishing this task, (2) what unconscious forces are being aroused as a result of this shift, and (3) what defenses are being erected to reduce anxiety. In effect, dreams provide the therapist with a perspective from which he can properly gauge which path he should pursue. At different times, the therapist's priority can make him attend to underlying anxieties, defenses against them, the patient's concern for the effect of her behavior on others, or the therapeutic relationship itself.

Therapeutic Goals

Freud was frequently asked the question, "How long should analysis take?" In response he would tell the story of a traveler in ancient

Greece. The traveler approached a man sitting by the side of the road and asked, "How far is it to Sparta?" to which the man replied, "How fast can you walk?" Goals in therapy are always patient oriented; no matter how skilled or ambitious the therapist, the patient ultimately will be the crucial determinant of whether treatment is successful or not. Therapeutic goals must be modified in accordance with certain givens: motivation, intelligence, extent of damage sustained during the formative years, powerful secondary gain factors that can make health a handicap rather than an asset, current environmental conditions, strength of the ego, and the capacity for insight and objectivity. In actual practice, the ideal goal of cure for every patient is not attainable. The realistic therapist tailors his treatment objectives in terms of the assets the patient brings to therapy. Practical goals include freedom from disturbing symptoms, the capacity to function reasonably well and to have some fun and happiness in life. Hopefully the patient will be as well adjusted as most people with whom she is in contact, which means that she may continue to be neurotic, although better able to live with her neurosis and to approach average life objectives.

Leopold Caligor and
Judith Caligor

The Dream in Psychoanalytic Therapy

Introduction

Freud's *The Interpretation of Dreams*, published in 1900, named the dream the *via reggia*, the royal road to the unconscious. Although much has been learned since then, and many more techniques and approaches have been tried, the dream continues to be at the very core of the psychoanalytic process.

When we talk of "dreams," we are referring to the conscious recall of a series of visual images perceived in the "mind's eye" while we are asleep. Our account of the dream describes the images and connects them with verbal explanations.

The dreams we recall have a different quality for us than our waking thoughts or experiences. There is more surprise, un-expectedness, difference from what we consciously know of ourselves and the way we behave.

The clinical understanding of this is that in sleep there is a "regression of the ego," a reduction in the censorship maintained in our waking hours, so that thoughts are permitted in our dream life that are not acceptable to our conscious minds. This suspension of censoring ceases upon awaking. The moment the dreamer wakes and recalls his dream, his defenses are mobilized to disguise, obliterate, or somehow distance the dream from his awareness. The awakened psyche cannot tolerate the dream in its primary form. The content tolerated by the ego while sleeping generates too much anxiety for the dreamer awake and so must be defended against.

The dream as reported is thus a product of the experience in the sleeping state and the psychological defensive structure that organizes it. When this is comprehended by the therapist, he obtains a cogent picture of what his patient is struggling with and how he is likely to try to protect himself, the essence of his personality organization.

Knowing this, many therapists will inquire about dreams in the initial interview with the patient. How illuminating this can be is illustrated by the following:

The patient, a twenty-five-year-old man, came to the therapist to talk about starting treatment. He came with concern about his fiancée, who was upset about what was happening in the relationship. He had had a series of broken engagements and didn't want it to happen again. In the interview the man was pleasant, cooperative, and responsive. Asked if he had had any repetitive childhood dreams, the patient reported that he had had many versions of the same two-part dream: he is in the kitchen or the living room having some pleasurable exchange with his mother. Then he is in his own room alone with a large Raggedy Ann doll, bigger than he is. He is twirling it around, throwing it against the wall; sometimes he rips off an arm. Inquiry further revealed that the patient's mother was very loving but very con-

trolling and demanding as well and that though the patient con-
formed on the surface, there was a huge well of rage underneath.

The division of the dream into two parts reflected the separate-
ness between the patient's conscious positive feelings and the dissociated rage he felt, which got communicated to women he became
committed to. It was to be a few years before this man was able to
comfortably come to terms with this and integrate it, but at this initial state of therapy it helped both the therapist and the patient to
understand the problem more clearly.

Psychoanalytic Theory on Dreams

People have been conjecturing about their dreams and their
meaning from the beginning of recorded history. However, the
foundation for our contemporary analytic understanding of dreams
was established by Freud's *The Interpretation of Dreams* (Freud
1953). This brilliant and complex work should be read by every
student of psychology, with the awareness that much of what seems
commonplace today was startling and original in 1900.

Freud contended that every dream owes its content to both past
and present—to early drives stemming from childhood as well as
drives seeking satisfaction in the present; that a dream is formed
when a current event makes contact with an experience from the
past; and that the content of the dream belongs to qualitatively different states of consciousness as well as to different periods of life.
Freud saw the manifest dream as a cryptic message that requires de-
ciphering, and he differentiated it from the latent dream, the ideas
and feelings underlying the manifest content. He posited that understanding the latent content reveals the wish fulfillment present in
every dream. The process by which the latent content is transformed into the manifest was called *dream work* and included the
major mechanisms of *condensation* (the compression of a number
of ideas into a single image), *displacement* (one person or part of a
person standing for another), and *symbolization* (an individual
selection of an object or creature to represent a set of ideas). The

dream work, the disguising of the latent dream thoughts, is a function of the ego. In dreams, pictorial metaphors express ideas. Spatial relationships are substituted for conceptual or temporal relationships.

As psychoanalysts gained their own experience in working with dreams, significant figures in the field formulated their differences with Freud's theory. This began early in the century when Carl Jung rejected the notion of wish fulfillment and childhood impulses as the source of dream content. Unlike Freud, who focused on latent content of the dream, Jung emphasized the manifest content as a source of true understanding. He said that he could not agree with Freud that the dream was a façade "behind which its meaning lies hidden—a meaning already known but, maliciously, so to speak, withheld from consciousness. To me dreams are a part of nature, which harbors no intention to deceive, but expresses something as best it can, just as a plant grows or an animal seeks its food as best it can." (Jung 1961, p. 161) Alfred Adler (1917), consistent with his approach to personality structure as a response to basic inferiority feelings, looked to the dream as a reflection of the dreamer's lifestyle, of his social and competitive strivings.

Maeder (1916), a follower of Jung's, elaborated the challenge to the rejection of the manifest content as only disguise data. He stressed its value in communicating the current psychological functioning of the patient.

Within the Freudian framework, Erikson (1954) extended Freud's formulations to include comprehension of the manifest dream. He warned psychoanalysts against discarding the manifest content, against mistaking "attention to surface for superficiality, and a concern with form for lack of depth." (p. 16) He postulated that the manifest dream includes a style of representation that is "a reflection of the individual ego's peculiar time space, the frame of reference for all its defenses, compromises, and achievements." (p. 21)

Theorists in the interpersonal school emphasized different aspects of the dream. Sullivan (1953) saw the dream as a parataxic distortion in the service of relief of interpersonal difficulties. He stressed that more important than finding cohesion in the dream elements is relating the dream to the current source of anxiety in the patient's life. Horney (1950) underscored the dream's potential for developing the patient's awareness of his real self, and Bonime (1962) added to this the dream as confrontation with his own identity in daily life. Erich Fromm (1951) stressed the dream's potential for revealing the patient's struggle to avoid responsibility for himself, his tendency to live out false solutions, while indicating hidden potentialities. Tauber and Green (1959) saw the manifest symbolic activity as important in its own right, permitting the patient to experiment and expand his self-concept. Caligor and May (1968) examined the development of basic personal symbols in the dreams of one patient during the course of a psychoanalysis. They demonstrated the reflection in the dream symbols of the growth in the self-concept and the ability to cope interpersonally. Ullman (1959) focused on the adaptive significance of the dream occurring in an experiential eye of inner vigilance and partial arousal. Committed to existential philosophy, Medard Boss (1958) emphasized the value of experiencing dreams to the exclusion of either studying them or interpreting them.

Overall, the trend in clinical practice has been to move from the sole emphasis on latent content in Freud's basic work to a major concern with the manifest content and the experience in the dream and associations to it as reflections of the patient's personality structure and functioning. The dream, then, is not only a pathway to repressed memories and historical happenings but an immediate communication of the current situation in the patient's functioning. With this it has become more feasible for the patient to become a more active participant in understanding and learning from his own dreams about his current as well as his past behavior. He is able to learn a style of thinking and approach to his problems in daily living with insights gained through his dream life. The unconscious motivations are understood and seen in relation to the patient's defensive structure and his current interpersonal behavior. The patient learns that through his dream he is stating something to himself

about his current incapacities that he somehow half knew but can
now confront.

Physiological Findings

Important research on the behavioral and physiological aspects of
dreaming is relatively recent.

In 1952, Aserinsky (1965), a graduate student of physiology at
the University of Chicago, noticed that throughout sleep people
show, periodically, rapid eye movements observed as darting eye-
ball movements under the closed lid and recorded on a polygraph
by means of tiny electrodes taped to the lid.

Further study revealed that these rapid eye movements were
clearly associated with dreaming in some way, as sleepers,
awakened during REM (acronym for rapid eye movements) sleep
were likely to recall their dreams whereas those awakened during
non-REM sleep tended not to recall their dreams.

Dement (1955) continued with research on these phenomena.
Connecting electroencephalographs with sleeping patients, Dement
verified that stages of sleep occurred in a predictable cycle. Stage 1
sleep, when the brain-wave pattern most resembled the waking
state, included the REM movements and probably the night's
dreams. He noted that REM periods compose about 20 percent of
the total sleep time.

Important to the clinician in this line of inquiry is the support for
the assumption that all people do dream regularly and that recalling
no dreams reflects that there are psychological processes inhibiting
the recall. The frequently observed increase in dreams as patients
proceed in therapy seems to be more dreams remembered rather
than more dreaming.

Working with the Dream in Therapy

Patients in psychotherapy are told that dreams are important to the
therapeutic process and should be reported when they are recalled.

This message is repeated periodically so that the patient becomes aware of the times that he is not remembering his dreams, or that he is not bringing them in to the therapy session.

When the patient does bring his dream in, the therapist notes the context within the therapy hour preceding and accompanying the reporting of the dream. The patient's mood, his interaction with the therapist that day, and the content of the material related before the dream is likely to be related to the dream.

The analyst also inquires about the happenings of the day preceding the dream, trying to get events or experiences, the "day residue," that triggered the dream.

After the dream is presented, the patient is encouraged to free associate to its elements, giving the feeling and memories evoked and gradually uncovering the underlying meaning of the dream.

The analyst actively participates with the patient in exploring the associations to his dream. He helps the patient to understand his ways of functioning with others historically and their relation to the current situation that has triggered the dream. Whatever difficulties exist for the patient in his life situation are reflected in the therapy and appear in the dreams. In this way the dream becomes the context for helping the patient to gain awareness of his present behavior.

As therapy proceeds, patients tend to remember more dreams and to recall them in greater detail. The attention to the dream from the therapist perpetuates and amplifies this phenomenon. Patients who do not recall dreams in psychotherapy usually have a therapist who is not particularly interested in dreams. For the patient who becomes accustomed to recalling and working on dreams, an extended period of not recalling a dream always marks a stage of resistance to the therapy.

The dream is always triggered by some happening in the present, but its core is historically based and reflects continuing conflicts or characterological adaptations.

An example of how disparate elements in the person's daily experience become connected with his past in the dream state follows.

A young man brought in a dream that he bemusedly reported as strange.

> "I was down at the harbor and a black Japanese ship entered and was destroying the American ships. I was terrified. I watched helplessly." In the course of the session the dream was explored and understood. The patient recalled that he had dreamed this on December 7 after he had heard a broadcast noting the anniversary of Pearl Harbor. That same day a Japanese man had been "coming on" to the dreamer's girlfriend. These happenings had been very much in the present, but associations to the feelings of terror and helplessness went straight back to the patient's childhood when he had felt betrayed by his father again and again—terrified of him yet helpless to defray the assault.

Frequently the transference reactions to the therapist are evidenced in the dream, giving the therapist an opportunity to help the patient express feelings toward him that he has been vaguely aware of but unable or unwilling to articulate. Illustrating this is the dream of a shy, constrained male patient who reported that:

> "My uncle and I were sitting on chairs perched on the wings of a plane. We were very comfortable. It was a bright, sunny day."
>
> Exploration of the dream led to the unique intimacy this man had had with his uncle. The contacts had been satisfying but very brief, as the uncle lived on another continent and an air flight was required for contact. The leisurely quality in the dream was difficult to manage in the brief visits they arranged. The bright sunny day symbolized the responsive, exhilarated response that this man had allowed in that relationship. It contrasted with the bored, distant feeling he had so much of the time. The patient gradually realized that he was experiencing some of the same good feeling in the analytic session but felt awkward about acknowledging it.

Although it is helpful and productive to get positive transference feelings to the surface, for many the dream is even more valuable as a reporter of negative transference. There is frequently more difficulty in acknowledging hostile, critical reactions to the therapist. For example, a patient who was particularly accommodating in her surface behavior with the therapist brought in a dream that puzzled her at first.

> She was alone in a room with a Nazi in charge of her. The Nazi commander cut her lip when she ventured to raise a question about procedures. This proper young woman was embarrased to acknowledge that angry feelings toward the therapist, the person in charge, had sometimes surfaced but were quickly put aside. This led to much more understanding of her behavior in therapy and the basis of her denial of hostility in the early relationship with a very rigid, conforming mother who became very anxious at any expression of aggression or rage from her child.

The most crucial issue in the dream is frequently its revelation of the central resistance to the treatment process and to growth in life. The dream provides a context within which the analyst can confront the patient with his conflicts and help him to awareness and to working through. The working alliance between the patient and the analyst is essential here both for the therapist's comprehension of the patient's dreams and for the communication of this to the patient. Resistance in the dream must be noted by the therapist and worked through if the patient is to experience and integrate the anxiety unleashed when his ways of defending himself in the dream are explored and brought to consciousness. Every dream a patient recalls during psychotherapy is in the service of the therapy. At some level, the patient wants cohesion to be made out of his confusion, for his distortions, evasions, and self-defeating resolutions to be challenged. As he learns to experience, tolerate, and integrate the attendant anxiety, he comes closer to being able to change.

The therapist's role in exploring the dream should be active. Resistance in the dream is coped with by the therapist's exploring with the patient, engaging him in the process, not by remaining silent or giving a monologue interpretation. In the dream, the therapist looks for the patient's ways of relating. These may be apparent or reflected only by omission, signifying a lack of adaptation. He notes what they portend for the patient in his present life and what they say about his self-concept and how it was formed historically. The therapist raises questions that stimulate and require the patient to respond and to participate in analyzing all aspects of the dream. The goal is to help the patient to confront himself. He is encouraged to see himself not as the helpless victim, but as the person actively doing, structuring the interpersonal field and evoking patterns of self-defeating responses in himself and others. The process should raise dissociated, unconscious aspects of patterned behavior into consciousness, so that the understanding of the behavior can be clarified and opened to modification. Without this awareness, the dissociated anxiety automatically takes over and triggers maladaptive behavior. The emphasis of the work with the dream is on understanding the defensive behavior, with, of course, the history of the maladaptive behavior being traced.

An example of this kind of clarification through the dream occurred in the therapy of a young woman patient. Without any real awareness of it, she tended to act rather superior and lofty as a way of dealing with her uneasiness and insecurity. This evolved naturally from her upbringing, which had constantly stressed social skills, signs of social superiority, and the importance of looking as if you had everything under control, while little attending to the development of the child's autonomy.

As her treatment progressed, she became more aware of some of her profoundly shaky feelings about herself; many experiences of childhood recalled very little feeling of confidence with family and with peers. The patient was struggling to comprehend this and integrate it with the ease she consciously experienced in the present. She brought the following dream to her session:

> I was swimming in the middle of a road. Then I saw big trucks bearing down on me. I was afraid I'd be squashed like an ant, so I climbed a tree. The truck drivers saw me up there and talked of chopping down the tree to get me down. I said, "Wait, if you'll just give me a hand, I can climb down myself." I thought, maybe I'll give them a few dollars.

The defensive structure delineated in this very lucid dream was apparent to the patient, though there was some surprise at the clarity with which it was spelled out. She was at a point in treatment where she was ready to relinquish her defensive distance. "Given a hand" she would come down to earth, be on the same level as others. She was shaky about it, however. The thought about tipping was a way of restoring the comfortable distance, underscoring social roles. Following the patient's associations led to feelings in her childhood of being miniscule, susceptible to obliteration. The following session the patient brought in further connections to the dream: Her sexual unresponsiveness and discomfort with men followed the same dynamics patterned in the dream.

As the patient and the therapist work on the dream together, following the patient's associations and attending to the feelings they summon in the patient, the transferential material and aspects of the self-concept that have eluded the patient come to the fore. Thus dream material, behavior with the therapist, and the current functioning that triggered the dream all converge. The reciprocity between intrapsychic and interpersonal behavior becomes apparent.

In the course of this exploration, the patient shares with the analyst shameful, unacceptable, or frightening material about himself. He permits himself to experience a relationship wherein he is valued and respected for this desire to grope, face his anxiety, and share his most sensitive and vulnerable feelings with another human being. It can be a moving and sincere experience for both. The patient is learning about a kind of intimacy with another person in which he finds out more about himself. This struggling through with another human being is a corrective emotional experience that promotes personal growth. The dream, through which the patient has the need to reveal himself and make contact with the therapist and yet to hide or cope in his characteristically self-defeating way, contributes centrally to the growing edge of the therapy.

As the patient proceeds through therapy, progress in his personal struggles are reflected in the symbols of his dreams. A symbol very frequently used in our culture is that of vehicles and their relation to passenger or driver. How a patient's progress was reflected in his dreams can be seen in the following series of three dreams in the two-year course of therapy of a young man who came to treatment in his late teens. He had grown up without a father and was dominated by an erratic and attention-demanding mother, quite isolated from peers. Soon after starting treatment with a male therapist he presented his first dream in treatment.

There was a little car, like a comic-strip car, its headlights bright, with a smiling mouth on the radiator grill. The car drives into a gas station. There was a friendly man near the pump. He filled up the little car's tank. As the gasoline went into the car, the car began to feel strong, and then suddenly had wings and soared off, happily, as the man waved.

This first dream revealed the young patient's wish to gain power in his new relationship with the therapist. The symbiotic relationship he had been geared to with his mother was transferred to his therapy. Underlying this were cravings for an infantile sexual relationship with the benevolent male figure. The childish quality of the dream reflected the gross immaturity of the patient at this beginning phase of treatment.

This dream was about a year later:

I was in a car with another person. I'm not sure if it's a man or a woman . . . both up front . . . I was the passenger. The driver kept going faster and faster. I was terrified that the car would get out of control.

The patient had been progressing toward differentiating himself and was beginning to define his sexual identity. He was working productively with his therapist and was feeling anxious about his dependency. Within his therapy he was recalling and reexperiencing panic he had had in trying to cope with his mother, who had been so controlling.

A year and a half later in treatment the patient brought the following dream:

I'm driving a bus, and the passengers are behind me. The bus is on open roads in the mountains. The bus keeps going faster and faster and is getting out of control. I feel panicked, but there is a man standing nearby who is not panicked. Although it's hard, I keep control of the bus, though it nearly runs off the road.

The patient is finding his own power, his autonomy, though he still has times when he is flooded with anxiety and fears losing control. The relationship with the therapist is providing some confidence.

In the progressive development of the vehicle image in these widely spaced dreams we can see a symbolic development of this young man from childish, symbiotic relatedness, through gradual differentiation, to an assumption of his own autonomy despite its precariousness and the anxiety it engenders.

The dream helps the patient and the therapist to progress beyond the cure that insight alone offers. Insight makes change possible. But the patient has to have living experience, both in the therapy relationship and outside of it, for change to take place.

The reader will note that sometimes one emphasis is more relevant, at other times another. The therapist's preference is based on an understanding of the patient's dynamics, the stage of therapy, and the patient's present difficulties. For example, in the discussion of the last few pages, salient aspects of different dream treatments were noted so that genetic aspects predominate in one and characterological in another, though both are always present.

The Dream in Short-Term Psychotherapy

Even when patients are seen only once a week for short-term psychotherapy, the dream can remain central to the understanding of core problems and underlying dissociated affects. The therapist works with the patient on relating the dream to current problems in the patient's life. Tracing the affects in the dream can vividly portray to the patient how problems from the past are relived in the present.

An example of this is a thirty-five-year-old blue-collar female patient who was seen for sixteen psychotherapy sessions once a week.

She had had an insecure childhood and adolescence, having been shifted through a series of foster homes. In the present, she demanded attention from her husband and complained bitterly of his neglect of her.

The patient reported the following dream: Her husband and she are in the kitchen and they are talking. She goes to put the coffee on the stove. She then turns around to find herself all alone and she experiences a deep burst of panic that awakens her.

Exploring the dream with the therapist, it became evident that this was the daily breakfast scene in the patient's life with her husband. The patient was able to identify the panic as her feeling when her husband left to go to work. She also recalled that this same panic was frequently experienced by her in the past when she had been moved from an already familiar foster home to a new setting. Further work with the dream helped the patient to understand her need for constant attention and her fears of neglect, which she experienced as desertion.

The Dream in the Context of the Therapy Session

To give the reader a better understanding of the place of the dream in the total psychotherapy process, we are including here a detailed account of an analytic therapy session in which a patient and a therapist work productively together.

The patient is a twenty-six-year-old attractive woman, well educated and doing responsible work. A presenting problem is her shyness with men. In the company of males she becomes flooded with anxiety, physically tense, and finds it difficult to talk and to think. The patient was raised by a mother who tended to be silent, unavailable, and easily flooded in contact. She had a brother several years older who was quite verbal, aggressive, and mocking, and with whom the patient could not compete. Her father, whom she experienced as loving, was ill at ease with people and seemed unavailable to the patient.

The therapy hour started with the patient coming in, seating herself, and appearing somewhat upset. When queried, she could give no specific reasons why. During the first ten minutes she seemed near tears, anxious, confused or diffuse, and avoidant. Attempts on the therapist's part to make eye contact or verbal communication were avoided by her. Her body was turned away from the therapist. Questions from the therapist were not responded to, muted into silences that she obviously found uncomfortable.

After a time the therapist asked the patient what she was feeling. When the patient answered that she was feeling scared and scattered but did not know why, the therapist urged her to "stay with the feeling." After a silence, the patient said, "This is a feeling I know I have often." After another pause, the patient spontaneously started to talk. She said that she had been out on a date with a man the night before. She described finding him attractive and bright, rather alive, and interested in her. However, as the evening progressed, the patient became shy and anxious. She was short of breath, and her thoughts were scattered. Her conversation was sparse, and the silences felt very uncomfortable. During this time the patient was not aware that she was feeling the same reaction with the therapist at that moment.

The therapist asked the patient to try to get back to that dinner last night and see if she could recapture this feeling. After a short period the patient stated that she knew she has had these feelings with men she likes, that this is a feeling she had during her childhood. She went on to say how painful silences had always been and how she blamed herself for them—how after a while she expected to be rejected or mocked, how she would get anxious and could not speak.

The therapist asked if she had had any dreams. The patient related the following dream: "It is dusk-like. I am in a boat with an oriental-looking man. He drives the boat into a dark area, an enclosed boat berth, and closes the door. It is near pitch dark. I am frightened that he will assault me. Suddenly there is a circle of intense light on the water. The light has dark dust specks throughout it so that I cannot see fully clearly. In the circle is a beautiful fish, trapped in the circle of light."

Asked by the therapist about the feeling in the dream, the patient answered, "fright." The therapist asked if anything had happened the day or night before the dream that comes to mind. The patient mentioned the date with the young man. (Note: As is often the case, the patient gives relevant material that makes the dream understandable *prior* to the dream, so that the dream gives the subjective perception of the reality the patient has experienced as well as significant historic data.)

The therapist then asked about the boat. The patient described that as an adolescent she had taken a boat ride with a boy who unexpectedly drove the boat into an enclosed berth and closed the door. It was dark, and she was panicked. He tried to get her to remove her bathing suit. She was frightened, and did not speak; although nothing happened, she was quite upset and avoided one-to-one contact with boys for a time afterwards. The patient spelled out that it was dark and she felt trapped, small. She was able to explore the feelings that the man was powerful, big (he stood over her), and she was small (seated), helpless, and felt trapped. She went on to say that she felt like that fish— trapped, looked at, unable to get away. The patient added, "fish cannot speak." (Note: The patient had had dreams of birds in cages with stuffed mouths—structurally quite similar to the fish in the circle of light: trapped, aesthetic, but helpless, inarticulate, isolated, and so on.)

The therapist noted that in the dream the man in the boat was oriental, and the patient recalled a birthday party during her childhood. There was an oriental man, a guest, who did not speak any English. He made Origami gifts for her—paper birds—as birthday gifts. His gifts were the most precious to her, yet he was strange and different. She knew he liked her, but she could not talk with him. She liked him but was frightened of him.

The therapist asked where she had experienced this before. The patient stated that she knew her father liked her; he was—is—loving, but there is never any real talk or contact between them. At that point there was an extended silence. The patient again became uncomfortable with the therapist. She flushed, appeared somewhat tense, and avoided eye contact; there was no talk. The therapist asked what the patient felt was going on between them. She described feeling frightened, and "I can't find words." The therapist wondered how she saw him. The patient said: "I know with my head that you are not hostile to me, yet I have this panic going on in me." The therapist encouraged her: "Good that you can experience panic yet have your head work. In the past, when this feeling would strike, its impact would be so strong that you could not think, and then there was no way out of the feeling." The patient said that she had always been terrified of this feeling. "I could never know why it happened or when . . . it would come and there was nothing I could do about it. I couldn't think, and my body would ache. It would just build up and not go away."

This was early in treatment, but there was an established relationship between this patient and the therapist. He understood her, she knew that and appreciated it, and he permitted a working alliance to form that was strong enough so that her irrational thoughts and inappropriate affects could be looked at by both of them together.

The therapist structured the session and the understanding of the dream in response to the mood and behavior with which the patient entered the session. He was aware of her heightened anxiety a discomfort with him. With this particular patient it was necessary to keep making suggestions to encourage her to express herself.

After the patient reported her dream, the therapist asked about the "day residue" to find out what triggered the dream, and then carefully explored her associations to the dream with her, both in terms of the content and of the affects.

Associations to the Japanese man whom she liked and feared and could not communicate with describe the transference relationship to the therapist in which she is reexperiencing early years with her father as well as the adolescent memory with the young man.

This transference reaction would be observed in the therapy session by the patient's tone of voice, her body movements, and her physical restlessness.

The image of the fish poignantly communicates to the therapist and to the patient some of her most personal feelings. She has selected the fish as her symbol; it is beautiful, yet in a primitive stage of evolving. Focused upon, it is trapped—inarticulate, looked down upon, and immobilized.

The patient came to encounters with men with these feelings and inevitably reexperienced them. Unconsciously the patient evoked a repetition of her fantasy expectations by her behavior.

In the therapy session work was progressing toward bringing this to awareness. The patient's ego capacities were getting stronger. Anxiety was no longer obliterating her capacity to think. She was learning to tolerate the anxiety and understand it better, preparing her to be open to new experiences outside of the therapy relationship.

Summary

This chapter presents a contemporary psychoanalytic approach to dreams in psychotherapy. The psychoanalytic approach is based upon contemporary understandings of ego psychology within the context of the parameters defined by the interpersonal school. The text presents the basic ideas of Freud, how these were modified through the century, and a description of how contemporary analytic therapists work with dreams and how this forms a central and integral part of the therapy.

George Stricker

Therapeutic Crises

A great deal has been written about crises (Bellak and Small 1965; Caplan 1964; Rosenbaum and Beebe 1975; Small 1972; Spiegel 1972), and many different approaches have been suggested. The literature in this area is rather disjointed and there is a good deal of disagreement on many points. Kalis (1970) has summarized what she feels are the consensual assumptions that have been derived by the various theorists about crisis. The assumptions begin with the statement that people generally achieve an equilibrium of functioning and will attempt to restore that equilibrium after any disruption. Some of these disruptions constitute crises states. During a disruption the person is more open to influence, and a disruption may be followed by a new adaptation. The equilibrium can be restored by a change in the environment, a change in the style of coping, or some combination of the two.

A crisis is always associated with a disruption of typical functioning and produces a disequilibrium in the individual. As such, it represents a turning point in the individual's development. It is marked by subjective discomfort and, if handled improperly, may lead to the development of severe symptomatology and increased pathology. More often it will last a relatively small amount of time, usually no longer than a few months, and the individual will return to her former state of equilibrium.

It should be clearly noted that the disequilibrium created by a crisis also produces an opportunity for a realignment of defenses and the establishment of a good deal of constructive growth. Usually people are frozen into a set pattern of functioning and any change requires a great deal of effort. When their pattern is unfrozen, the opportunity exists to realign this pattern in a very constructive direction. There probably is no time that an individual is as open to positive change as in the midst of a crisis, despite the severe discomfort that is being experienced. After the crisis is resolved and equilibrium is restored, the individual is likely to be frozen once again, either into her characteristic means of functioning or, if the situation has been well handled, at a higher level.

Not every crisis is an emergency, and the therapist must be sensitive to this distinction. An emergency is only one type of crisis and it requires immediate action on the part of the therapist. In some cases, the failure to act immediately might result in a suicide attempt or an acute psychosis. In other cases, the therapist need not act as quickly; but if a crisis prevails, there still may be a need for a typical functioning by the therapist so as to take advantage of the patient's potential growth, to avert the potential for increased pathology, and to reduce the immediate distress.

We can look at the circumstances that create disruption as falling along a continuum. At one end of the continuum is the traumatic event. This is a situation that is so catastrophic in nature that it is likely that any individual experiencing it would undergo a disruption in functioning. These can include events such as the death of a loved one, a fire, or the discovery of a life-threatening illness. At the other end of the continuum lies a precipitating event that appears to most observers to be trivial. The impact of the event is due to a heightened state of vulnerability in the patient that is brought about by an internal dynamic factor. The closer the precipitating event falls to the traumatic end of the continuum, the more responsive the patient usually will be to treatment. It may seem paradoxical that the most successful treatment is in the situation that appears to be least trivial.

In a traumatic situation the patient may have a very sound ego that was understandably overwhelmed by a powerful external event. Restoration of equilibrium to the prior level of functioning is sufficient, and the patient has many resources with which the therapist can work. On the other hand, when a crisis develops in response to minor stimulation, we are dealing with a person whose prior equilibrium was fairly brittle and whose ego resources are likely to have been strained to the breaking point. In the first instance, the therapist might be content to restore the previous level of functioning with a relatively brief intervention. In the latter case, the previous level was not at all adequate and much longer and more intensive treatment is indicated.

Fenichel (1954) has made clear that the two general approaches to dealing with crisis situations take apparently contradictory directions. The first of these approaches involves attempts to escape from the trauma, and includes an armamentarium of supportive techniques. The second involves attempts to master the trauma, and includes techniques that stress catharsis and abreaction. The therapist should have both techniques at his disposal and attempt to find the proper combination. It should be noted that there is no necessary relationship between the type of treatment and the type of onset. Thus, whether a crisis was precipitated by a trauma or a trivial event does not indicate whether supportive or cathartic techniques should be utilized, and either may be useful with both types of occurrence.

The supportive approaches often include a degree of activity on the part of the therapist that is unusual for a psychoanalytically oriented practitioner. Dependency needs of the patient are gratified by the increased attention of the therapist, and this serves to reduce anxiety. It is often important to let a patient in the midst of a crisis know that the therapist will be available, at least by telephone, at any time. Many patients undergoing crises will experience a great deal of comfort and relief from this knowledge, even though they do not make use of the privilege that is offered.

The therapist might also choose to offer intellectual guidance to the patient in order to help her to cope with a stress situation. Providing information about such matters as the physical consequences of masturbation or the appropriate treatment of venereal disease may help a patient to see a difficult situation in a more realistic light. Converting the anxiety into a form where it can be dealt with intellectually places emphasis on an ego function and thereby helps to strengthen the ego. We must remember that in supportive therapy it is the ego of the patient that is being supported. The general support and encouragement of constructive ego functions is particularly valuable in times of crisis, and it also helps to increase the self-esteem of the patient.

Even neurotic defenses might usefully be supported in time of crisis. The patient is in the midst of a difficult situation and priorities must be established. It is more immediately important for an obsessional patient to handle a disruptive flood of anxiety created by a threat of divorce than it is to abandon obsessive mechanisms. Thus, if such a patient can begin the process of finding an attorney and making constructive plans for the arrangement of her life, these intellectual defenses may serve to reduce her anxiety to a manageable proportion. At a later time the negative aspects of intellectualization can be examined.

The therapist may even intervene and directly manipulate the life situation of the patient, particularly in times of emergency. For example, the therapist may meet with family members and instruct them as to which of their behaviors are appropriate and which are destructive for a patient who is experiencing an extreme crisis. Each of these supportive activities on the part of the therapist will foster positive transference and increase the patient's belief in the magical healing powers of the therapist. While this will require analysis at a later time, it is a valuable tool in dealing with the immediate situation.

One of the interventions that falls at the cathartic end of the continuum is an encouragement to reexperience the initial precipitating event. This may mean the recall of a real occurrence, such as witnessing a fatal accident, which created a good deal of pain. With repeated exploration it may be mastered, and the ego will be strengthened by doing so.

Another interaction involves the uncovering of feelings that have been repressed and that place a great deal of strain on the individual's functioning. For example, becoming aware of anger can be very helpful to a person who had gone to great lengths to avoid recognition of this feeling. It would not be unusual for a depressed person to feel a good deal better after being able to recognize and express her hostility to a significant object in her life. However, this is not an area that is to be approached lightly. The very presence of strong defenses against the recognition of feelings indicates the difficulty that the patient has with them, and their expression; while it may produce immediate relief, it may also lead to a good deal of guilt and further symptomatology. Thus, it is often important for the therapist to mediate the catharsis. If the therapist can present both sides of the patient's ambivalence, and express and justify the negative feelings, the patient is likely to be more comfortable in acknowledging them. In some types of impulse disorder, the therapist must also be careful that the catharsis does not precipitate acting out of the impulses with a decided negative consequence to both the patient and the object.

A further form of catharsis may occur when a patient begins to speak about previously forbidden topics, acknowledging that it is possible to feel angry with a parent or to feel sexually attracted to the spouse of a close friend. The recognition that the therapist is not punishing this feeling can lead to some relief. Further, as forbidden feelings are expressed, connections among them and other occurrences can be established, and the ego will be strengthened by the achievement of greater control in these areas.

It is clear that the therapist requires a greater degree of activity in the event of a crisis than in usual day-to-day functioning. But it is important to recognize that the active participation of the therapist does not necessarily mean taking over direct responsibility for the conduct of the patient's life. It is far preferable for the therapist to use the activity in order to support the assets of the patient, to add strength to the patient, and to encourage the patient to travel in a direction that has already been set. While the therapist is more active, as much as possible the patient should provide the resolution for the problem. If the patient is able to resolve the problem for herself, with the support of the therapist, this will increase the patient's self-esteem and sense of mastery and add to the strength of the ego. It will also promote positive transference, which can be useful in later stages of treatment (although it will also add an unrealistic quality to the transference that will need to be examined). On the other hand, if the therapist takes direct and personal responsibility for the resolution of the crisis, the patient may increase her belief in the therapist's magic, but is also likely to experience added dependency and a sense of loss of autonomy. In some emergency situations it may be necessary for the therapist to take direct charge, since the resources of the patient have been depleted. However, as quickly as the patient is able to resume responsibility for her own functioning, the therapist must give up the position of omnipotence and return autonomy to the patient.

One of the most important skills that the therapist has in dealing with crises is the ability to make a rapid and accurate diagnosis. Diagnosis does not refer to classification within a particular nosological category, but rather to an assessment of the dynamics and resources of the patient, and a full appreciation of the events that gave rise to the crisis. This often will require very careful and very detailed questioning, and the therapist does not have the usual luxury of time in acquiring information about the patient. Not only is the eliciting of detailed information helpful to the therapist in arriving at a diagnostic formulation, it also can be a supportive technique in that it adds a measure of structure and control to the interview that probably will provide reassurance to the patient and a semblance of rationality in a situation that the patient feels has gotten out of control.

The accurate assessment of the patient's resources and defenses often will provide the therapist with the proper direction for his interventions. It is interesting to note that some resolutions to crisis situations may take the form of artificial substitute symptoms. Glover (1931) has noted that these artificial symptoms may often substitute for spontaneous symptoms and make the more noxious symptoms become superfluous. Thus, a patient who is told not to engage in a certain kind of behavior can be seen as being given an artificial phobia, while the patient who is given specific advice as to detailed means of handling a situation has been presented with an artificial compulsion. The choice of intervention will depend on the knowledge of which defense is most congenial to the patient. Let us take the case of a patient who is flooded with unacceptable angry feelings toward her employer. If it is clear that we are dealing with a person with obsessive-compulsive defenses, we might suggest a number of cognitive acts that will prove useful in this situation. Thus, the patient may be encouraged to keep a careful list of the times that she has felt this way, and the specific events that gave rise to the feelings. On the other hand, this is likely to be a very ineffective intervention with a patient who has severe problems with impulse control. In this case the therapist might suggest that the patient immediately leave the room and engage in some type of recreational activity that will displace the anger on to a neutral ob-

ject. The target practice at a pistol range that will be helpful to the
impulse disorder would not have been helpful to the first patient
with her obsessive-compulsive defenses.

Let us consider the relationship between the crisis and the remainder of the treatment. In some cases a crisis will occur in the course
of ongoing treatment. In other cases a crisis will precipitate the
patient's seeking of treatment, and the first part of therapy will in-
volve dealing with the crisis. It is likely, for some patients, that the
therapy will consist entirely of dealing with the crisis, and when the
patient's equilibrium is restored, the need for treatment will no
longer be felt. Where the crisis was precipitated by a genuine
trauma, the need for treatment may be dubious after the crisis has
been resolved. Even when there is a need that is clear in the therapist's mind, the patient may not choose to follow through.

Whether the crisis occurs at the onset of treatment or in the midst
of treatment has a great deal of impact on the behavior and resources of the therapist. If the crisis is at the onset of treatment,
there will be need for a great deal of careful history taking so that
the diagnostic impression can be formed. When the crisis occurs in
the midst of treatment, it is likely that the therapist will already
have achieved a dynamic understanding of the patient, and the only
careful questioning that will be required will surround the actual
events leading to the development of the crisis situation.

At the beginning of treatment, a patient is likely to have very
little transference attachment to the therapist other than the magical
powers endowed on the healer. The patient is likely to feel particularly dependent because of her immediate need, and this will ac-
celerate her belief in the curative powers of the therapist. When a
crisis occurs at a later point in treatment, the transference will be a
great deal more complicated and will depend on the specific details
of each case.

A very important difference concerns the implication for the
balance of the treatment. When the crisis begins the therapy, there
may not be any further treatment, depending upon how circum-

scribed the patient feels the problem to be. However, if treatment should continue, it will be with an extreme positive transference and an irrational belief in the power of the therapist, along with an expectation that the therapist will continue to behave in the very active way that has characterized the handling of the crisis. When the therapist abandons the extraordinary activity, this is likely to create excessive frustration and will provide an issue that must be handled. When the crisis occurs in the midst of treatment, its successful resolution will add to the positive transference, but this will be tempered by the patient's previous experience with the therapist. The reversion to a less active approach may not be as frustrating, depending upon the dynamics of the individual patient. However, in both cases there is always the danger that the patient will produce crises in order to increase the activity level of the therapist and satisfy dependency needs. If this threatens to become a pattern, it must be recognized early and dealt with rapidly.

Up to this point, a general approach to crisis and emergency situations has been described. Regardless of the specific event, a careful diagnosis is necessary and the therapist will have both supportive and cathartic techniques available. In the remainder of the paper, some specific types of crisis will be explored, and some specific approaches will be described that might be indicated or prove to be useful.

One relatively common crisis that is particularly frightening surrounds the possibility of suicide. This can include a fleeting thought of suicide, a more careful suicidal plan, an active suicidal gesture, or an actual or completed suicidal act. Since suicide is so serious an event, it always demands careful attention. Suicide is almost always preceded by some planning on the part of the patient, so it behooves the therapist to pay careful attention to any material in this area. On the other hand, the therapist must be careful not to overreact or to institute emergency procedures where they are not required by the situation. A careful diagnostic formulation will separate the fleeting thought, or even the chronic obsessive preoccu-

pation that is unlikely to be acted upon, from the serious probability
of self-destruction.

It is trite to repeat that a thought about, or gesture toward, suicide represents a cry for help on the part of the patient. It should
be clear that this is a cry that the therapist should heed. To ignore
it risks allowing the situation to escalate, and also encourages the
patient to cry even louder. If the report of loneliness and wishes to
be reunited with loved ones, and fantasies about how others will
act after one is gone, do not succeed in mobilizing the therapist,
then perhaps some active suicidal attempt will. A patient who is a
suicidal risk has usually experienced a severe loss. The loss may be
actual, as in the case of the death of a loved one or a loss of health
or status, or it may be a symbolic loss, such as a clear indication
that aspirations will not be fulfilled. In any case, the loss is followed by a reduction in self-esteem, a feeling of loneliness and helplessness, and a lack of energy and enthusiasm. The availability of
the therapist is very supportive to a patient who feels the world
crumbling around her. The activity of the therapist, which may be
in sharp contrast to the therapist's usual behavior, is an effective
counterpoint to the patient's feeling of energy depletion and may
encourage the patient to borrow the therapist's ego and achieve
some vicarious sense of being alive.

It is important for the therapist to understand the specific dynamics of each suicidal patient in order to be able to help the patient
to reach that same understanding and to arrive at a more effective
solution. The expression of the feelings associated with the suicide
can often serve a very helpful cathartic function. Other than depression, the major affect that the patient usually experiences is aggression, although this aggression is often directed against the self
and not perceived consciously. The therapist can help the patient to
achieve some catharsis, but this should be through the technique of
mediate catharsis, so that the brunt of the burden need not be felt
by the patient. An untempered expression of anger may lead to a
violent outburst on the part of the patient, but often will lead to

later feelings of guilt and unworthiness. Thus, the therapist should assume some responsibility for the aggression by expressing it for the patient and presenting it in a sanctioned light. It is also helpful to express the other side of the patient's ambivalence, which also helps temper the intensity of the feeling. For example, rather than encourage a patient to express the resentment she feels toward her dying husband who has become a burden to her, it is much more helpful for the therapist to indicate how frustrating and frightening it must be for the patient to have to care for him, particularly when she has loved him so much in the past and now sees him as a shell of his former self. This allows the anger to be expressed in a far more appropriate and sanctioned context than if it were expressed in its raw form.

Any activity by the therapist that serves to raise the lowered self-esteem of the patient is very helpful. Reassurance often is useful in this regard, but it must be appropriate and understandable. The therapist who describes how capable and competent the patient is, while the patient is feeling anything but, is likely to be seen as just one more person who has been taken in by the façade, and any further likelihood of such an insensitive therapist being of help is discounted. It might be more reassuring to indicate to the patient that her thoughts and her actions are separate. Thus, it is acceptable to be angry with someone because she need not follow through with violent action. Since she has been successful in restraining herself from violence in the past, it is likely that she will continue to be successful in doing so. This thought will be reassuring to the patient, will strengthen the patient's ego as it feels a sense of control over the situation, and is much less likely to be discounted.

The increased activity of the therapist in the case where suicide is threatened is a very important component of the intervention. The patient should be told how to reach the therapist at all times, should be invited to make use of the therapist, and should be carefully told that the therapist should be called before the patient undertakes any suicidal activity. The use of adjuncts to treatment, such as medication and hospitalization, must also be carefully considered. These will be dealt with in more detail later in the chapter. The threat of homicide represents a severe crisis, although it is a very unusual one. While some obsessional patients may talk at length about their violent fantasies, these are unlikely to be acted upon and usually do not constitute a crisis. The more the patient presents a history of impulsivity and violent action, the more seriously one must take any indication that homicide is imminent. In some instances the impulse is frightening and egodystonic, and this should be capitalized on by the therapist.

Two types of patient at risk for homicide present different combinations of anger and fantasy. One person experiences anger directly, without any fantasies that serve to reduce the intensity of the affect. The other can have a rich and elaborate fantasy, but has this isolated from any feelings, so that a breakdown in the defense will flood the patient with anger and lead to an acting out of these fantasies. In both cases the homicidal behavior will be preceded by loss of control, and the major focus of the therapist will be on activities that will help restore control.

In cases where the patient feels out of control and subject to the whims of her impulses, the therapist often can intercede between the patient and the impulse, lending his ego to the patient for the time being. In some cases, forbidding the patient from acting on the impulse will be useful, although this cannot always prove effective. In cases of real danger, the therapist may recommend an alteration in the patient's environment, so that the patient will leave a job or a home that is stimulating her anger. In every case the therapist will act to oppose impulsivity. One way of doing this is to underline whatever feelings the patient has about the behavior being egodystonic and adding whatever new information might serve to produce such an attitude. An appeal to narcissism may occasionally be helpful with a person who regularly acts out. While she may not experience any guilt about the consequences of her activity, she may recognize the purpose of restraint as a means of avoiding a prison sentence, and she may also understand that beating her child will only lead to a more severe judgment against her in any subsequent divorce action and recognize the greater wisdom of restraint.

Any movement in the direction of delay will strengthen the ego and oppose impulsivity. One technique is to encourage the patient to call the therapist, rather than to take action, whenever she feels the urge to do so. The telephone call may be cathartic, and certainly will postpone any activity, since it is impossible to act murderously while speaking on the phone. As much as possible, the therapist should separate affect from action. The patient should recognize that feelings need not be expressed in behavior, and it is appropriate to be angry at someone who has wronged her without necessarily taking immediate revenge upon that person.

It is tempting to help the patient to express anger verbally, but this is a very dangerous technique with patients whose controls are limited. It is important that cathartic activities in therapy do not serve to give the patient license to act out. In every case, the expression of the anger should be accompanied by cautions against its translation into action.

A further method of ensuring control is to direct the patient away from any stimuli to the loss of control. Chemical stimulants such as drugs and alcohol must be avoided by patients with impulse disorders, since they only serve to weaken the ego and increase the likelihood of acting out.

There is an important legal issue that the therapist dealing with potential homicidal behavior must be aware of. In a recent decision by the California courts (*Tarasoff* v. *Regents of University of California* 1974), it was held that the therapist who is informed that a patient has homicidal plans against another individual, and believes those plans are likely to be acted upon, must warn the intended victim or be held liable. This creates enormous complications in terms of the usual confidentiality of the therapeutic relationship, and also poses a very difficult problem because of the questionable likelihood of accurately predicting homicidal behavior. While this ruling is relevant only in California, it may well have precedential value in other jurisdictions. If a therapist intends to behave in conformity with the Tarasoff decision, it is his responsibility to so indicate to the patient, so that the confidentiality contract will be stated accurately at the beginning of treatment and need not be violated.

The therapist may occasionally be confronted with an acute psychotic reaction, either in a new patient or in the course of treatment. When dealing with psychotic patients, it is important to behave in a manner that will strengthen the ego of the patient, encourage secondary process thinking, and help the patient restore her former equilibrium. In many cases, the therapist may have to intercede his ego and lend it to the patient to compensate for the patient's own weaknesses. This is an instance where supportive therapy will be undertaken as a temporary measure to restore functioning.

One of the prime functions of the ego is to deal with reality, and this function must be supported. Any reality distortions on the part of the patient, either of inner feelings or external events, must be corrected, and any inappropriate behaviors on the basis of these distortions must be prohibited. Limit setting is particularly important, and may be effective if a strong positive transference has been established. The therapist must respond in a firm and highly structured manner, and use the weight of his authority to control the patient's behavior.

In attempting to understand the patient's situation, it is important that the therapist recognize the affect as well as the content that is being expressed. To argue with a paranoid patient about the reality of a delusion is a useless endeavor. On the other hand, to recognize the anger or fright that underlies the delusion, and to help the patient to clarify these inner feelings, will add to the adequacy of reality testing and serve to strengthen the ego of the patient. Naming a feeling or an occurrence is a very primitive means of mastery, and giving the patient some intellectual recognition may be a way of adding some order to a frighteningly disordered world.

In the event that these activities on the part of the therapist are not successful, then the use of external controls will have to be considered seriously. These include medication, which often is remarkably helpful in acute psychotic states, and also hospitalization, which provides continuing external structure and also removal from the precipitating circumstances. Often the time given to the patient by a brief hospitalization will allow for a reintegration, and then treatment can continue on a more effective basis.

Not every patient who seeks out a therapist in a state of disorganization is experiencing an acute psychotic reaction. For this reason, the establishment of a clear and accurate diagnosis will dictate the appropriate intervention. In some cases, the patient will be experiencing an acute panic state. The panic will occur when the patient is unable to function as she ordinarily does, and finds herself flooded by anxiety. A remarkable variety of symptoms can be presented in these circumstances, but the common feature is the expression of anxiety or its symptomatic equivalent, accompanied by the feeling of vulnerability, helplessness, and inability to cope. The diagnostic appraisal is important, not only in differentiating this condition from psychosis, but also in aiding an understanding of the precipitating event.

In the case of a panic reaction, catharsis in a safe and protected atmosphere is very helpful. The patient's expression of her fears occurs in the company of a supportive and reassuring therapist. Some of the tension will be discharged and the patient will achieve a greater sense of mastery over the situation. The ability to give words to feelings is important in reducing the intensity of the feeling and bringing it under the control of the ego. It is not likely that any single cathartic session will eliminate the panic reaction. However, it will endow the therapist with a semblance of effectiveness, and encourage the patient to seek out the therapist when further panic seems incipient. The therapist must be available to the patient at such times, and the patient's knowledge that the therapist will be available often will help to forestall a panic reaction. Since the patient feels vulnerable and helpless, the encouragement of functioning in areas of mastery will add to the esteem of the patient and also strengthen the ego. The patient will ordinarily be tempted to withdraw from all activities because of the panic, and in doing so will further strip herself of any sense of esteem or confidence.

To the extent that the patient can understand the circumstances that brought about the panic, the mastery of the anxiety will be hastened. The panic may be brought about because of such varied dynamic factors as feelings of uncontrollable rage, stimulation to unacceptable heterosexual behavior, and temptation toward homosexual behavior. If the patient can be helped to understand this specific dynamic precipitant, this will set the stage for later mastery of the conflict. Even though the panic can be eliminated through removal from the precipitating situation and strengthening of the ego, the patient will still be prone to further panic when similar situations recur.

In some cases, a panic reaction or a depressive reaction will occur in response to a genuine traumatic event. It may be the death of a loved one, the discovery of a terminal illness, the experience of a catastrophic environmental event such as a fire, participation in wartime activity, or any number of such events. If these occur in an otherwise well adjusted individual, the therapist should be able to help the patient by providing some distance from the trauma and an ability to master it. It is important that the patient achieve a full expression of the attendant feelings and a catharsis. The repression of the feelings of anger, fear, loss, and so on will provide a fertile ground for later symptom development. As with other panic reactions, a catharsis should be achieved in a setting where support and reassurance can be provided. Although each trauma has its own specific characteristics and each patient her own peculiar dynamics, the general principle that will hold is to seek a full expression of feelings in a supportive atmosphere, and to accompany this with an ability to achieve distance from the trauma and intellectual mastery over it.

There are a number of crises that occur unavoidably in the course of development. Predictably, most individuals will begin school, undergo puberty, leave home, marry, have children, occasionally divorce, and frequently have to deal with the loss of loved ones. In some instances these crises will produce acute symptomatology that will be dealt with in a manner similar to that described for the panic reactions. More often the symptomatology will be less flagrant and there will be no need for any extraordinary measure. It is not unusual for an adolescent to enter treatment because of problems of separation or identity formation. These are issues that represent a developmental crisis and provide the therapist with a very good opportunity to help the patient achieve significant growth. However, they do not often require the institution of emergency procedures, and treatment can be undertaken in a more traditional manner.

There are a number of adjuncts to treatment that the therapist can invoke. These are most useful in the case of true emergencies and will help the therapist to impose control and restore order. Foremost among these methods is the use of drugs. There are a great many drugs that are available for the reduction of anxiety, the control of psychotic symptomology, and the elevation of mood. The therapist should be familiar with the nature and effect of these drugs, their possible side effects and contraindications, and their limitations. It is very helpful to have access to pharmacotherapy where it is indicated, and it is equally important not to rely on an artificial crutch when the patient can be helped to achieve mastery through the strengthening of the ego. In instances where drugs are not sufficient to control the emergency situation, hospitalization must be considered. The therapist should be aware of the resources that are available in a community and should be willing to make use of them when necessary. A brief hospital stay will always remove the patient from the immediate environmental stimulation that has contributed to the problem, and will often provide necessary external structure and control. The hospital should not be looked upon as magic, and the goal of treatment is the reintroduction of the patient to the environment when she is able to master it.

A further adjunct involves the active intervention of the therapist in the life circumstances of the patient. This will include such measures as instructing family members as to how to behave with the patient and directing the patient as to situations to be sought out and others to be avoided. This active intervention reduces the autonomy of the patient and should be done only when necessary, but it will often be useful in providing the patient with both additional time and the relaxation of pressure so that autonomy can be restored.

The diagnostic importance of recognizing and responding to crisis and emergency procedures has been stressed. The other side of this coin is the recognition of pseudoemergencies. These are situations that are presented as though they require immediate intervention, but in fact they do not. While it is possible to conceive of all crises as resistances, since they require atypical therapist behavior and divert the usual flow of treatment, the pseudoemergency can be most clearly conceptualized and handled as a resistance. The pseudoemergency represents a demand for help on the part of the patient. The therapist should recognize that help is being requested, but may prefer to assist the patient in seeking means of fulfilling these needs other than their direct gratification. A patient who demands additional sessions whenever she is faced with a decision will be helped more if she recognizes her dependency needs than if the therapist meets them, although she will also be made more anxious. The dynamic implications of the presentation of pseudo-emergencies must be fully explored, but the demands need not be fulfilled.

The focus of this chapter has been crisis intervention. However, a word is also in order concerning crisis prevention. A prepared ego is always better able to cope with a situation than one that is taken by surprise. The therapist who is working in an ongoing relationship may achieve an understanding of the patient that will allow him to be able to anticipate circumstances that will present great difficulty. Alerting the patient to these circumstances and rehearsing some appropriate responses may help to take the edge off the crisis and allow the patient to achieve mastery without experiencing disequilibrium. In any case, following the resolution of a crisis, it is always helpful to explore the situation in retrospect so that the patient may learn from one painful experience in order to avoid a second one. A patient can be helped to recognize the external and internal cues that precede a crisis. These cues can then be responded to at an earlier time and in a more effective way if they recur.

A further approach to crisis prevention involves the anticipation of developmental crises. Thus, such activities as premarital counseling, preparing a mother for her reaction to the birth of her child, or preparing a child for the impact of a future sibling, will often serve to reduce the severe impact that such a potential source of disequilibrium can induce.

A few words must also be added about the therapist. Up to this point this chapter has assumed that the crisis occurs exclusively in the patient, and that the therapist can function in an effective manner in dealing with this crisis. Occasionally the therapist will experience a personal crisis, and this will have impact on all his ongoing therapeutic relationships. Therapists also get married, have children, separate from their families, and lose loved ones. When such events occur, they often will be reflected in the treatment that the therapist can offer. In less extreme cases, the therapist may wish to share this part of himself with the patient so that the patient does not feel personal responsibility for the therapist's ineffectiveness, insensitivity, or impatience. This expression of humanity on the part of the therapist may often be valued by the patient and will promote a sense of equality and partnership that will help to strengthen the ego of most patients. In some cases, the dependent or narcissistic patient will have no concern for the problems of the therapist. This too will be helpful in providing immediate material to be explored within the relationship. In situations where the therapist's disruption is more extreme, either supervision, additional personal therapy, or even the cancellation of sessions or transfer of patients may be indicated.

When the crisis is being experienced by the patient, the therapist will often have countertransferential responses. These may take the form of feelings of omnipotence or of helplessness, of fright, or of overinvestment. The therapist must recognize that he will do all that he can, but that there are some limitations upon his functioning. The frightened therapist may withdraw from the patient at the time of greatest need. The omnipotent therapist may glory in taking over the life of another person, and relinquish this power with great reluctance. As is always the case with unconscious countertransference, it represents a source of interference in the treatment and should be mastered through the therapist's own supervision or treatment.

Dale H. Ortmeyer

End Phase of Treatment

Introduction

Therapy stops because conditions make it impossible to continue or because the work is finished. The former, which gets spelled out in any number of practical conditions and/or effective resistances to further treatment, will be called premature termination of treatment. The latter implies the goals of treatment have been met. Ending then occurs as a process that continues to promote awareness until the dyad dissolves. This end phase or process is an important and distinct stage of treatment. It will be discussed in terms of both long-term and short-term therapy.

The psychotherapeutic techniques of dream and fantasy analysis, correction of parataxic distortions in present and past experience (Sullivan 1953), accurate recall of immediate experience, and free association are common to the total treatment process, including the end phase. What is unique in the end phase is that the intention of leavetaking is clearly spelled out before it occurs,* with a mutually shared agreement to look at its complexity in the patient's life. The intention is both threatening (anxiety provoking) and challenging to growth (self-actualizing); it invariably involves anticipated loss, and actual loss once the intention is a reality. It can occur too soon or too late in the treatment process. An important part of termination is its mobilization of memories, fantasy, and feelings attached to present and earlier losses. Considerable effort is spent in ensuring that the ending is not traumatic, allowing for continued self-use of psychotherapeutic understanding once the treatment process is ended. The discussion that follows is organized around these thoughts about the end phase of treatment.

Certain words of explanation are voiced here about a view of the total treatment to more precisely convey what is meant about its endings. One needs to assess and to treat the total personality in its tension-reduction and its self-actualization aspects (Singer 1965). The interplay of these two motives occurs at every step of treatment. Therefore, it is not sufficient to analyze distortions and to reduce anxiety. It is equally important to facilitate the actualization of enjoyment, satisfaction, and new experience.

It is vital to differentiate reality experience from fantasy. A doom-forecasting fantasy such as "all is lost" or a fear of death must be separated from the mourning of the ending of the dyad. The other people in the room are the patient's unconscious fantasy projections. They need differentiation from the therapist, to whom they are fused in the transference. The differentiation allows the patient to readmit his projections into his personality to integrate. Once readmitted, the patient can pursue on separate mental tracks the reality of experience and illusion (fictive selves). He, in turn,

---

*This seldom occurs in endings in day-to-day living. Behavior rituals tend to mask and render unconscious the varied notions of endings.

views the therapist more realistically as an egalitarian ally with limitations. This in no way is meant to disapprove of illusion. On the contrary, inner fiction in the form of imagery or thought is the wellspring of creative approach to experience. Play (Bruner 1976), which partakes much of fantasy life, is most important for learning. It maximizes enjoyment and is clearly not committed experience, for which there is considerable consequential risk. The clarity of separating fantasy from reality, as Winnicott (1965) indicates, allows challenge and variety in each of these two personality dimensions. These comments about treatment in general apply also to the end phase of treatment.

Selected Review of Literature

The current practice of psychoanalytically oriented psychotherapy has three major themes that differ from those of therapy of a few decades ago. These themes enter every phase of therapeutic work, particularly the end phase. First, an egalitarian, sharing model based on collaborative effort has replaced the authoritarian model where the doctor prescribes (Havens 1973). The therapist is more a consultant than a master builder. It is particularly in the end phase that egalitarianism is apparent. It is to be achieved between patient and therapist even though the patient earlier in the therapy demanded a prescription for thoughts, emotions, and actions. The therapist, furthermore, is held responsible for resolving counter-transference reactions of an authoritarian nature. The date for ending, the analysis of dreams and transference, thus become as much a responsibility of the patient as of the therapist in the end phase. It need not necessarily follow, of course, that the patient and the therapist become friends after treatment is finished. Ideally, friendship after treatment is possible. Practically, it does not often happen. A variety of factors, such as differing lifestyles, preclude friendship. The fantasy of becoming close friends in the end phase is seen both as pleasurable and as an avoidance of loss at ending.

This change to egalitarianism seems largely due to the increasing awareness of the culture-based nature of personality, styles of thinking, and emotional expression. Egalitarianism is not necessarily present, of course, in present-day authoritarian cultures.

Second, particularly in the end phase, the drive-reduction model of motivation has been supplanted by a combination of tension-reduction and self-actualization. Emotional health is not only the reduction of anxiety. It is equally the actualization of new skills and new challenges. The end phase is particularly infused with the search for new challenges. Pleasurable time is spent in relating such experience during sessions. The already considerable awareness of anxiety-provoking patterns reduces the necessity of character analysis.

Third, the character of a patient and his interpersonal inner patterns are the problematic area for therapeutic work. The traumatic theory of neuroses with only childhood causes behind symptoms has become less significant as a model. Pattern and structure, interpersonal and intrapsychic, present and developmental, are the unconscious contents brought to awareness along with or rather than childhood trauma. The end phase is particularly a time to explore again or newly become aware of unfortunate interactional and intrapsychic patterns. The fallibility of a validated (scientific) reconstruction of the past from adult memory is in part responsible for the speciousness of a traumatic theory of neuroses. The reconstruction is rather a shared mythology between patient and therapist, not a scientific validation of childhood experience (Schecter 1976). The mythology is valued extremely highly, however, as a necessity for learning intimacy. It is the model of the intimate empathic experience of mother-child. The myth of trauma and "bad" parents leaving one embittered and scarred is replaced by the myth of accepting the limitations of one's parents and childhood. The latter leaves one more free to fully experience the present.

Only brief mention will be made here of Freud's, Greenson's, and Sullivan's positions on the end phase of treatment. Freud (1913) likened the ending process as analogous to the end game of chess, where the moves are predictable and finite. Note that such a statement has an authoritarian, prescriptive flavor. In his (1937) last excellent paper on treatment, he had a much more cautious and culture-bound orientation to termination. For example, he states that the analyst cannot have *one* notion of psychic normality. His theory, throughout his writings, was drive-reduction motivated. It was Hartmann, Kris, and Loewenstein (1946) who brought self-actualization into Freudian theorizing with the notion of the conflict-free sphere of the ego.

Greenson (1967), following the Freudian conceptual framework, does not discuss in detail the ending of treatment. He does make a vigorous point regarding termination and transference. He maintains that our present-day, more complete understanding of child development makes it vital to analyze the transference hate as well as the transference love. Transference hate is the unresolved hate of parental figures of the past projected onto the therapist. Greenson maintains that intense and prolonged hateful reactions toward the therapist should emerge once a working alliance is established. These reactions need to be analyzed before there is termination. He states that: "The interminable analyses, the negative therapeutic reactions are, in my experience, invariably examples of insufficient analysis of the transference hate." (1967, p. 236)

Sullivan's (1953) criteria for termination were: The patient must know himself as much the same person as he is known by others. The consensual validation of self and others' appraisals implies the *awareness* of parataxic distortions (illusions). Elsewhere, he said: "A person achieves emotional health to the extent that he becomes aware of his interpersonal relationships." (Chapman 1976, p. 224) Sullivan *shared* responsibility with his patients for goal-achievement leading to termination. Note that this is an egalitarian position. He was not oriented toward a traumatic theory of neurosis. Rather, he looked for inner interpersonal patterns that distort present interpersonal involvement.

Premature Termination of Treatment

Premature termination occurs when the therapeutic relationship stops before the goals for change are realized. For conceptual clarity, premature termination is separated into (1) the practical conditions that necessitate termination, (2) resistances in the ongoing treatment that result in termination, and (3) the brief process involved in premature termination.

The practical conditions requiring termination can, of course, be of many varieties. There is an implicit suggestion in much of the psychoanalytic literature that any premature termination is the result of unresolved resistance or transference. This seems to the author an authoritarian notion. Can patients control their lives over a considerable period of time to ensure continuance of their therapy? In our present-day, complex urban living, people's life situations can change rapidly, for better or worse. This is not to say, of course, that resistance should not always be evaluated when premature termination occurs. The practical conditions under consideration here were not known at the beginning of treatment. If they were, then the goals of treatment would be arranged into brief psychotherapy, counseling, or some form of short-term treatment.*
Under discussion here is long-term and intensive treatment. By long-term we mean longer than a year, and intensive suggests twice a week or more. The long-term nature of treatment cannot preclude practical interferences. One does not stop living because one is in therapy. On the other hand, one looks closely at practical considerations for differentiating their reality from their transference possibility. Premature termination also does not include patients who stop after a few sessions. Here a working alliance has not had time to develop. What is terminated is the inability to share anxiety-provoking experience in the dyad.

The practical conditions of premature termination revolve around (1) change in income or payment, (2) change in life situation, and

---

*Ending of short-term therapy will be discussed later.

(3) change in therapist's work. An ever-present possibility in many patient's lives is loss of job or loss of major source of income. A patient seen by the author, for instance, had been relieved of his job due to economy cuts at his place of work. He became depressed and passive. Therapeutic effort was aimed at working through his depression and his regaining an assertive effort to resume his profession. In the meantime, his bill to the therapist kept mounting even though the fee and frequency of sessions were reduced. As his depression lifted, he decided to terminate treatment because his debt kept increasing. He spoke to the therapist occasionally thereafter by telephone, and he regained professional employment. His new work involved a considerable cut in income. He did not resume treatment since his income was cut. Lowered income and accrued debts shifted his options for spending his income. Such instances remind therapists that they are dispensable. The issue of resistance was looked at, but not felt to be valid here. In another instance, a woman was divorcing her husband and had no source of income other than alimony and child-support payments. She decided that, in the priorities of her life, the basic necessities for her children and herself came before continuing in therapy. In these particular instances, economics rather than resistance seemed 'to be the major factors in termination. In our present-day living, such considerations are more common than not.

Changes in life situation often occur as a result of the therapeutic helpfulness. A woman in therapy may be able to develop an intimate relationship for the first time, but her boyfriend or husband is transferred to another geographical area. She then has the real struggle of going with him and terminating therapy before she is ready to do the latter. A man may work through his neurotic work inhibitions. The ensuing success leaves him traveling so much that therapy can no longer be meaningfully conducted.

Therapists, particularly those in the process of establishing themselves, often change their clinic jobs, or their status within a training institute, or other jobs. They then may not be able to continue with their patients. A therapist in a clinic, for example, advanced from a full-time therapist to assistant director. He had to relinquish half of his patient load. Another therapist graduated from a training institute and moved so far away that she could not see her patients. In the above situations, termination is primarily a result of life changes of patients or therapists, not resistance to further therapy. There is often discussion of resuming treatment in the future if life situations permit it. The patient may be helped to find another therapist in the geographical area where he plans to live. In numerous instances there is resumption of therapy. In others, there is not. If the environment is sufficiently facilitating for the latter patients, as Winnicott (1965) says, they may indeed continue effectively on a self-helping basis. If not, it seems doubtful that they can continue in their growth toward intimacy and independence.

There are, of course, instances in which termination occurs due to resistances. One such kind of termination is when neither therapist nor patient is aware of a distortion operating. The patient then acts out the resistance by ending the treatment. Another occurrence is when the therapist is aware of such distortion coming from the patient, but her own countertransference is sufficiently intense to prevent her from resolving the neurotic bind. A third situation is when both patient and therapist are aware of the resistance, but it is so persistent or dramatic that the patient cannot resolve it except by termination. A fourth instance is when the patient is working through a character pattern and becomes very tense. Convinced he is worse, he leaves treatment.

In the first-mentioned instance of resistance, there is lack of awareness by both patient and therapist. How is this known? It can become apparent in supervision. It can also be discovered by either the therapist or the patient long after termination has occurred. The patient may see someone else for therapy. Through further therapy, he becomes aware of the irrational expectations he had of the previous therapist that did not allow him to continue. The therapist sometimes finds out from a colleague that a former patient of hers has resumed treatment. She hears what is happening in their therapeutic work. Rethinking her own therapeutic work and termination с/ith the patient, she perceives resistances not previously seen. The author, for example, supervised a young male therapist who was seeing a very attractive, seductive young woman. He had considerable tension as to his sexual attraction to her not-so-subtle advances. He was not aware of and therefore could not interpret her attempted seduction as a mask for considerable fear of and anger toward men. She eventually terminated therapy with the rationale that she had found a boyfriend and did not need further therapy. Some time later she reentered therapy with a colleague of the author's, after her boyfriend did not work out. She went through an extended angry reaction to men, including the previous and current therapist. It would appear that the patient's inability to become aware of her hatred of men (see Greenson 1967) was then acted out by her leaving her first therapist.

In another supervisory instance, a patient was very provocative, intimidating, and angry with his therapist. The therapist became inhibited, fearful of the patient's potential violence, and could not effectively set limits for him. Not insisting that the patient look at his projected fear of her allowed him to be intimidating. Termination occurred by referral to another therapist. Here the therapist was aware of the distortion, but was too intimidated (countertransference) to manage the neurotic communication.

In a third instance, the author had worked with an hysterical patient over a lengthy period of time. She was helped in resolving many of her fears and inhibitions. Both of us were aware in the latter part of treatment of her inability to resolve her conflict regarding her mother. She had had a most difficult relationship with her mother and could not resolve her feelings around her mother's untimely death. Each time the patient approached this area of her inner life, she became so intensely anxious and symptomatic that further exploration was suspended. Termination occurred with awareness of this unresolved, troublesome area of her inner life, but no resolution.

A fourth instance can occur when a character pattern begins emerging *into awareness*. The patient feels more anxious. If the anxiety is not interpreted as progress in the analysis of the patient's problems, he usually assumes he is getting worse. An example comes to mind of a patient who was fearful of succeeding. As he worked through his fear of success, and indeed became more successful in his work, he became most anxious. He acted out an old pattern of following accomplishment by passivity and inhibition in order to cope with increased anxiety. The anxiety revolved around an expectation of criticism and rejection that he still projected onto his superiors. The perception of his increased success generalized to an expectation of success in all areas of his life. He thereby entertained the notion that he was cured. The latter belief inhibited him from being open about his inner fears. It was only with considerable insistence by the therapist that he describe in detail his fears about his workaday life that he began to understand his dilemma. He said later he was about to terminate treatment, convinced he *should* feel better but in fact feeling worse.

What are the salient aspects of the brief process involved in premature termination? Above all, the therapist needs to be realistic. If she feels there is unfinished business, or inability to go further, she ought to say so. She should define, as clearly as she can to herself and her patient, the circumstances of the leavetaking. She expresses her opinion about what is left undone. She may well express her own feelings about the leavetaking, and most certainly elicits the patient's feelings and thoughts. Most important, perhaps, there is an active discussion of what has been accomplished. If not, the patient in prematurely leaving is likely to color the whole therapeutic experience with negative feelings. Such feelings tend to mask the benefits derived. This denial and negative attitude can render the whole experience meaningless.

The author recalls an experience of premature termination with a patient that illustrates this brief process. A young woman whom the therapist had seen in therapy for about a year came to a session announcing at its beginning that this was her last session. She related this not-so-startling bit of news in a matter-of-fact way as though talking of the weather. We both knew she had a longstanding pattern of leaving relationships abruptly, including previous therapeutic ones. She had earlier in therapy talked of stopping, but had never carried it out. There had been considerable probing of this leavetaking, but it was not clearly understood. The author was startled when he realized, after her repeated statement, that she meant what she said. Now there was a determination in her voice and repeated words that convinced the author of her leaving. With the realization that she meant to leave, the author felt annoyed. He told her that she had some nerve in announcing this to him in the way she did. She, of course, had a right to stop seeing him. He resented her unwillingness, however, to let him in on the decision, let alone examine the validity of it. He also told her with feeling that he would miss her. She became upset but maintained her position. She agreed with him in the remainder of the hour to look at what help she had received, and what problems she still had. This was quite meaningful, and at parting she had tears in her eyes. About a year later, she came in for a session to tell the author how meaningful that last session had been to her. What she had found particularly helpful was his insistence that she look at what was occurring. She particularly remembered that her behavior was a rejection and a denial of the importance of the therapeutic relationship. This knowledge had allowed her to continue using what she had learned in therapy.

Ending Short-Term Psychotherapy

Ending short-term psychotherapy is both similar and dissimilar to premature termination and ending long-term psychotherapy. Except for free association, the psychotherapeutic techniques previously mentioned are common to short-term therapy, including the end-phase. The associative technique, both in its acquisition and in its utilization, requires greater time and leisure than that afforded in fifteen to thirty sessions. The short time period in treatment implies three major distinctions from premature termination and ending of long-term psychotherapy.

First, the awareness of treatment ending is part of the total treatment, not just the end phase. Such awareness does not permit a leisurely search for relatedness and does not allow tackling many issues of intimate involvement. It leaves the therapist and patient much more in role relatedness, which does not allow an egalitarian involvement. The ending, therefore, can often have a glow or halo effect since the great diversity of relatedness, including negative interaction, need not occur. Neither do the roles, resembling characters in a game or a play, become divested of their mythology. It thereby also becomes easier to substitute others in the roles at future times, should such become necessary.

Second, working through the mourning or loss aspect of ending is largely absent. There has not been time in treatment to work through clearcut distinctions between fantasy and reality in relatedness. The patient, with little or no awareness, utilizes the particular automatic fantasy formulation available in his past life to deal with ending. The endings, therefore, can be very diverse but without much thoughtful insight into change. One patient can depart, experiencing a happy occasion filled with gratitude and appreciation for help given. Another can have repressed negative feelings, and leaving can be acted out by breaking final appointments or by arriving very late. A third patient experiences anger at not being allowed to continue, and transfers onto the therapist or the whole therapeutic experience his negative feelings. In any one instance of leavetaking, the therapist ought to reflect with the patient the mode of the leaving as a challenge for the patient to think through on his own. There is not the time in treatment, however, to work through the ending with insight and change.

The author has worked as a therapist for several years in short-term therapy with blue-collar workers. In one instance, a patient was most appreciative upon leaving treatment. He experienced relief from anxiety around a conflict with his boss and his wife. The therapist shared the patient's good feelings, noted the positive way the patient dealt with leaving, and introduced a word of caution upon a possible return of the conflicts and anxiety. Over a number of years, this patient has been back to see the therapist for four periods of short-term therapy. Each time, the patient has left on a very positive note, seeing no need to continue. The patient has no wish to look into such a leavetaking pattern, nor would he do so. In several other instances, patients have canceled or broken last sessions, always for seemingly plausible reasons. Such a pattern of leavetaking is not uncommon in our culture. It helps one to avoid looking at conflicting feelings and to evade an estimation of help received. The angry departure is the third cited instance above. It is rarer, and shows more courage than does avoidance. It is an attempt to address the nature of the loss and the limitations experienced with the departure. It is done, unfortunately, in a negative and rejecting mood, leaving residual feelings of guilt. There can be resultant repression of what help has been received. Here an acceptance of the right of the patient to feel anger and loss is important; but it is also important to differentiate it from the reality of the help, however limited, that has been received.

Finally, short-term therapy is focused or goal oriented and is therefore more task specific than long-term therapy. Once the goal is realized, the notion of termination occurs rather than a thoughtful perusal of expanding the possibility of help. If the goal is not quickly reached, there is a search for other modalities of therapy, such as long-term therapy, to deal with the problems at hand. The patient previously mentioned, who had four short-term therapy experiences with the author, came in initially with acute anxiety. The anxiety quickly became connected with a power struggle with his boss over just and unjust working conditions, and a similar struggle with his wife around "who wanted sex, when, and where." Utilizing the projected roles of the "powerful doctor" and the "willing patient," suggestions were made that allowed more effective and reasonable interactions to occur. As this happened, the patient was relieved and left on a happy note despite some protestations from the therapist. In each return to therapy, the central focus was similar. This man was not educated in or oriented to insight. Upon improvement of his interpersonal field, he felt fine and refused further involvement. The endings occurred pleasurably, allowing the possibility of further focal treatment, but with no insight into the nature of the ending.

Ending Treatment and Goals

As was mentioned earlier, the issues of termination and goals are intertwined. Goals in long-term treatment can be a diagnostic statement early on in the work. So often, however, the goals change or are unclear until well along. This is to be expected because motivation for further or continued help builds as a patient experiences change in himself. Goals often change in a patient's mind; for example, from symptom or mood relief to change in character. The therapist may have goals in mind early in the treatment, but not know if they can be effected. Goals inevitably become important in the therapist's and patient's minds as the issue of termination arises. Where we've been and what is left to do is posed. The dialectic between goals or expectations and the reality of what occurred is a powerful style of thought the patient can utilize long after treatment ends. It implies future expectations and the way toward continued growth.

The author suggests a general statement as to goals in psychoanalytically oriented psychotherapy. The proposal is that one brings *sufficiently* to the patient's awareness *unfortunate* character patterns so that when they occur in specific situations the patient is able to become aware of the familiar refrain, to stop it, and to substitute more effective alternatives. The crucial words here are sufficiently and unfortunate. *Sufficiently* involves not only awareness of character, but the experiencing of the relief and satisfaction of alternative and more effective ways of coping with anxious situations. *Unfortunate* refers to character patterns primarily used to reduce anxiety. These patterns are relatively rigid in nature, and thus do not permit other options. In the long run, they are self-defeating, and elevate anxiety. The process of becoming aware of the familiar refrain, of stopping it, and of substituting more effective alternatives is at issue in termination. When this process keeps recurring in treatment with minimal help from the therapist, then the issue of termination is certainly pertinent. Please note, however, that termination is not a decision of the therapist's. The decision lies with the patient. It occurs when he, by and large, no longer needs the therapist in order to become aware of unfortunate patterns as they occur in specific experiences in his life.

An example comes to mind, stated very briefly, of a woman in her early forties whom the therapist has seen for some ten years. She falls into the currently much discussed group of patients called *borderline*. She has been able to resolve a number of difficulties in her life around sex, marriage, meaningful employment, and the establishment of the friendships she desires. Recently she has been able to relate incidents that in past times would have left her detached and confused. Now she becomes anxious. Labeling her anxiety, she has demanded of herself to think of what is happening. She has then shifted her tension level and her behavior. For example, she became most anxious when another woman strongly criticized her effectiveness in a group where she is the leader and the other woman a group member. The patient's initial reaction was one of inner panic. She then recounted being aware of her anxiety and of stopping the old pattern of detachment, withdrawal, and inability to talk. She related this to her mother's unrelenting criticism when she did well. The patient was then able to label the other woman's jealousy of her leadership ability. She was able to maintain her own effective charge of the group. She has been able to become aware in many such situations, and alter the old, unfortunate patterns with minimal help from the therapist. Such capability has led both of us to raise the possibility of termination.

The Process of Termination

The question posed here is: termination of what? Certainly not of an inner dialectic of the ever-present ambivalence in humankind. Not awareness of the inner experience the patient continues to have. Not of a thoughtful way of perceiving anxiety, conflict, and dreams. Not of the understanding of symbolism in dreams and fantasy as it applies to one's current and future life. For it is not sufficient to work at the intellectual game of dream interpretation. Dreams, the heart of our visual imagery and symbolism, need translation into our everyday life as well.

Neither is there a cessation of a continued appreciation of the richness of one's family and cultural heritage. There is not an ending to the continual challenge of direct, intense, and lively inner experience of emotion and a comfortable yet meaningful interpersonal expression. There is not a termination of a continued satisfaction in the understanding of the personal myths, family myths, and cultural stereotypes that are part of oneself. The whole range of imagery, thought, and feeling is not lost. It is kept available for recall in one's mind's eye.

It is vital during this phase of treatment that the therapist share with the patient the pleasure of the positive growth of the patient. It is just this positive growth that the patient often denies in his anxiety and ambivalence about leavetaking.

There is, of course, a termination of the therapeutic relationship. This means a loss or mourning process that needs to be explored in the final phase of treatment. The process, for purposes of conceptual clarity, is discussed in four aspects.

First, there is the mourning for the unfortunate character patterns of the neurotic self. These patterns have been called the transference projections of the past, which lead to current interpersonal problems. Sullivan (1953) says that the parataxic distortions from past unfortunate patterns of behavior with significant others must be sufficiently given up so that one can more or less see oneself as others do. While Sullivan does not emphasize the loss aspect, the function of awareness of the parataxic projection is to allow the loss and correction to occur.

As one formerly hysterical patient said in her final phase of treatment with the author (Ortmeyer, in press):

I see now that my intense desire for a happy life completely filled with affection and sex and gratification is possible only in my private fantasy world (parataxic distortion). When I start demanding this gratification of myself and my husband, I'm in real trouble. My intense frustration and anger is primarily in relation to my ideal. It leads to contempt for the all-too-human weakness I see in myself and in my husband. When I project this demand on my husband, I am only discontent with him. It comes up in so many subtle ways. I'm catching myself now, and saying to myself, "Oh, that's my trouble." Then I can relax better again and deal more effectively with whatever problem is facing me. I expected that of you [the therapist], too. I used to feel so frustrated and disillusioned when you didn't make everything all right for me. Now I see more clearly when you're way off. At times you're distracted and don't remember what I say. It's not so bad now. I'm relieved that you're human, too. But it's so hard to give up the fantasy. I still cry myself to sleep sometimes—at least I know what I cry about now—when my husband is all caught up in himself or cold to me.

Second, the process of termination involves a mourning of the real relationship with the therapist. This is an experience of sadness. It is equally a feeling of liberation and freedom. There is the exciting prospective challenge of being on one's own. After all, the never-ending mastery of complex, learned social skills and inner thought is an exciting challenge. True, it may at times be lonely. The rewards, however, are of confidence and independence.

A third important aspect of the process of termination is the pursuit of previous experiences in the personal history of the patient where leavetaking occurred. It is necessary to go into these past experiences in some detail, or for review if they were previously worked through. The awareness is needed of exactly how defensively or directly the patient has dealt with this important aspect of human relatedness. Here is the time to look at the patient's concerns about loss and death. It has been the author's experience that therapists have trouble in this area of treatment.

It is most important that the therapist have clearcut distinctions between leavetaking and "fear of loss or death." The patient looks to the therapist for a realistic way of dealing with leavetaking. Directness, nonavoidance, and appropriate but not undue emotional reactions are vital. This means the therapist has been able to deal realistically with leavetaking and mourning in her own life, and is aware of her own fantasy fears about death or loss.

A referent point for the therapist here, consistent with the rest of the therapy, is: Who are you in the projections or transference of the patient? The history of the patient is pursued with this transferential focus. The formerly hysterical patient just mentioned had a most narcissistic father who realistically offered her very little in love or discipline. He did offer her, however, a fantastic fantasy of what a great father he was by his own consistent verbal admission to her as such. This was designed to make her eternally admiring of and grateful to him. In the final phase of treatment, I worked through with her that I did not care for her admiring offerings to me (transference). I did care for and respect her capabilities, which allowed her to be truly free and independent of me when we terminated. Another example of history of leavetaking comes to mind in the person of a formerly very obsessional and schizoid man who was in the final phase of treatment. He was eager to be free of the therapy, to go his own way and spend his money elsewhere. At the same time he was frightened and sad at the prospect. He had also regressed to detachment and angry denunciation of me. As the leavetaking history was pursued, he recalled with very strong emotion what earlier in the treatment he had been able to reveal only in passing. He was able to disclose the impossible leavetaking with his father. His father was a schoolteacher who had an excellent reputation as a friendly and dedicated educator of children. The patient believed this image of his father, and held himself at fault for the great difficulty of his father's relationship with him. His father, for example, would start working with the patient on a project. He would quickly get impatient and angry if the patient made mistakes. He would then not explain what he expected the patient to do. He might ridicule his son for being stupid and completely do the project himself to show his son how to do it correctly. Through this the patient would get anxious, furious, outwardly control it, then afterward feel humiliated and utterly useless. He remembered having nightmares and fantasies of death for his father. This unfortunate pattern would go on daily. The patient would have crying jags with his mother. By about ten years of age, he avoided his father, never going to him for help, and fearing and hating him. His father, in turn, was embittered. The patient went through a daily loss of self-esteem and of effective functioning. This was not helped particularly by his turning to his mother for solace, and being called a sissy by his father. The patient was able to relive and work through this difficult pattern in the final phase of treatment, when leavetaking was imminent.

A final and very frequent occurrence in termination is the patient's temporary regression to old symptoms, to old mood states, and to old interpersonal problems. The patient typically experiences this as becoming worse again. This is often accompanied by a reproach to the therapist for terminating prematurely or not helping the patient, or by the patient's suggesting the need to change to another therapist to finish the treatment. The all-too-obvious message is: "I need to continue treatment since I'm not well enough to be on my own." The transference pattern here is typically the parent or parents who figured most prominently in the patient's fantasies, anxieties, and realities concerning abandonment. The therapist, of course, must actively interpret the abandonment anxiety theme in relation to the reality of the termination of the therapeutic relationship, of the patient's current real-life situation, and of the emotional reliving regarding parents. The interpretations flow into a review of the patient's life and the therapeutic experience. The preparation here is for a continued growth in inner experience and outward expression for an indefinite time beyond termination of the actual therapeutic relationship.

References

Adler, A. (1917). A study of organ inferiority and its psychical compensation. *Nerv. ment. dis. Monogr. Ser.*, No. 24.

Aserinsky, E. (1965). Periodic respiratory patterns occurring in conjunction with eye movements during sleep. *Sci.* 150: 763–766.

Balint, M. (1950). Changing therapeutic aims and techniques in psychoanalysis. *Int. J. Psycho-Analysis* 31: 117–124.

Bellak, L., and L. Small (1965). *Emergency Psychotherapy and Brief Psychotherapy.* New York: Grune and Stratton.

Berman, L. (1949). Countertransference and the attitudes of the analyst. *Psychiatry* 12: 159–166.

Bonime, W. (1962). *The Clinical Use of Dreams.* New York: Basic Books.

Boss, M. (1958). *The Analysis of Dreams.* New York: Philosophical Library.

Breuer, J., and S. Freud (1895). Studies on hysteria. In Strachey, J. (ed.) (1953), *The Standard Edition of the Complete Psychological Works of Sigmund Freud*, 2. London: Hogarth.

Bruner, J. S., A. Jolly, and K. Sylva (Eds.) (1976). *Play.* New York: Basic Books.

Caligor, L., and R. May (1968). *Dreams and Symbols.* New York: Basic Books.

Caplan, G. (1964). *Principles of Preventive Psychiatry.* New York: Basic Books.

Chapman, A. H. (1976). *Harry Stack Sullivan.* New York: Putnam.

Cohen, M. B. (1952). Countertransference and anxiety. *Psychiatry* 15: 231–243.

Dement, W. (1955). Dream recall and eye movements during sleep in schizophrenics and normals. *J. nerv. ment. Dis.* 122: 263–269.

Dollard, J., and N. Miller (1950). *Personality and Psychotherapy.* New York: McGraw-Hill.

Eisenbud, R. (1977). Value conflicts between women therapists and women patients. *Clin. Psychol.* 30: 14–17.

Erikson, E. H. (1950). *Childhood and Society.* New York: Norton.

_____ (1954). The dream specimen of psychoanalysis. *J. Amer. Psychoanal. Ass.* 2: 5–56.

Fenichel, O. (1941). *Problems of Psychoanalytic Technique.* New York: Norton.

_____ (1945). *The Psychoanalytic Theory of Neurosis.* New York: Norton.

_____ (1954). Brief psychotherapy. In Fenichel, H., and D. Rapaport (eds.), *The Collected Papers of Otto Fenichel: Second Series.* New York: Norton.

Fisher, K. A. (1976). *The Guru Therapist's Notebook.* Garden City, N.Y.: Adelphi University Press.

French, T. M., and F. Alexander (1946). *Psychoanalytic Therapy.* New York: Ronald.

Freud, A. (1946). *The Ego and the Mechanisms of Defense.* New York: International Universities Press.

Freud, S. (1900). The interpretation of dreams. In Strachey, J. (ed.) (1953), *The Standard Edition of the Complete Psychological Works of Sigmund Freud,* 4 and 5. London: Hogarth.

_____ (1905a). Fragment of an analysis of a case of hysteria. *Standard Edition,* 7, 3–122.

_____ (1905b). On psychotherapy. *Standard Edition,* 7, 257–268.

_____ (1910a). Five lectures on psychoanalysis (transference and resistance). *Standard Edition,* 11, 49–58.

_____ (1910b). The future prospects of psychoanalytic therapy. *Standard Edition,* 11, 139–151.

_____ (1910c). "Wild" psychoanalysis. *Standard Edition,* 11, 219–227.

_____ (1912a). The dynamics of transference. *Standard Edition,* 12, 97–108.

_____ (1912b). Recommendations to physicians practising psychoanalysis. *Standard Edition,* 12, 109–120.

_____ (1913). On beginning the treatment. *Standard Edition,* 12, 121–144.

_____ (1914a). Remembering, repeating, and working-through. *Standard Edition,* 12, 145–156.

_____ (1914b). Fausse Reconnaissance (Déjà Raconti) in psychoanalytic treatment. *Standard Edition,* 13, 201–207.

_____ (1915). Observations on transference-love. *Standard Edition,* 12, 157–171.

_____ (1916–1917). Introductory lectures on psychoanalysis. *Standard Edition,* 15 and 16.

_____ (1920). Beyond the pleasure principle. *Standard Edition,* 18, 3–64.

———— (1923). The ego and the id. *Standard Edition, 19,* 3–66.

———— (1926). Inhibitions, symptoms and anxiety. *Standard Edition, 20* 77–175.

———— (1932). New introductory lectures on psychoanalysis. *Standard Edition, 22,* 3–182.

———— (1937). Analysis terminable and interminable. *Standard Edition, 23,* 209–253.

———— (1938). An outline of psychoanalysis. *Standard Edition, 23,* 141–207.

Fromm, E. (1951). *The Forgotten Language.* New York: Rinehart.

Fromm-Reichmann, F. (1950). *Principles of Intensive Psychotherapy.* Chicago: University of Chicago Press.

Gitelson, M. (1952). The emotional position of the analyst in the psychoanalytic situation. *Int. J. Psycho-Analysis* 33: 1–10.

Glover, E. (1931). The therapeutic effect of inexact interpretation. *Int. J. Psycho-Analysis* 12: 397–411.

———— (1955). *The Technique of Psychoanalysis.* New York: International Universities Press.

Greenacre, P. (1950). General problems of acting out. In *Trauma, Growth, and Personality.* New York: Norton.

Greenson, R. R. (1967). *The Technique and Practice of Psychoanalysis,* Vol. 1. New York: International Universities Press.

Hartmann, H., E. Kris, and R. M. Lowenstein (1946). Comments on the formation of psychic structure. *Psychoanal. Study Child* 2: 11–38.

Havens, L. L. (1973). *Approaches to the Mind.* Boston: Little, Brown.

Heinmann, P. (1950). On countertransference. *Int. J. Psycho-Analysis* 31: 81–84.

Horney, K. (1950). *Neurosis and Human Growth.* New York: Norton.

Jones, E. (1953). *The Life and Works of Sigmund Freud,* Vol. 1. New York: Basic Books.

Jung, C. (1961). *Memories, Dreams, Reflections.* New York: Vintage Books.

Kalis, B. L. (1970). Crisis theory: Its relevance for community psychology and directions for development. In Adelson, D., and B. L. Kalis (eds.), *Community Psychology and Mental Health: Perspectives and Challenges.* Scranton, Pa.: Chandler.

Kaplan, D. M. (1971–1972). On transference-love and generativity. *Psychoanal. Rev.* 58: 573–579.

Kaplan, H., M. Sadock, and A. Friedman (1975). Erik Erikson. In Friedman, A., H. Kaplan, and M. Sadock (eds.), *Comprehensive Textbook of Psychiatry, 1,* 566–573. Baltimore: Williams and Wilkins.

Kernberg. O. (1976). Transference and countertransference in the treatment of borderline patients. In *Object Relations, Theory and Clinical Psychoanalysis,* Chapter 6. New York: Jason Aaronson.

Klein, M. (1952). The origins of transference. *Int. J. Psycho-Analysis* 33: 433–438.

Krasner, L. (1962). Behavior control and social responsibility. *Amer. Psychologist* 17: 199–204.

Langs, R. (1973). *The Technique of Psychoanalytic Psychotherapy.* New York: Jason Aaronson.

Lazarus, A. (1971). *Behavior Therapy and Beyond.* New York: McGraw-Hill.

Little, M. (1951). Countertransference and the patient's response to it. *Int. J. Psycho-Analysis* 32: 32–40.

Maeder, A. E. (1916). The dream problem. *Nerv. ment. dis. Monogr. Ser.* No. 22.

May, R. (1958). Existence: A new dimension in psychiatry and psychology. In May, R., E. Angel, and H. F. Ellenburger (eds.), *Existence.* New York: Basic Books.

Meeks, J. E. (1975). *The Fragile Alliance.* New York: Robert Krieger, pp. 82–110.

Menninger, K. (1958). *The Theory of Psychoanalytic Technique.* New York: Basic Books.

Ortmeyer, D. H. (in press). Interpersonal psychotherapy with the hysterical character. In Goldman, G. D., and D. S. Milman (eds.), *Parameters in Psychoanalytic Psychotherapy.*

Perls, F., R. Hefferline, and P. Goodman (1965). *Gestalt Therapy.* New York: Dell.

Reich, A. (1951). On countertransference. *Int. J. Psycho-Analysis* 32: 25–31.

Reich, W. (1928). On character analysis. In Fliess, R. (ed.) (1948), *The Psychoanalytic Reader, 1,* 129–147. New York: International Universities Press.

Reich, W. (1929). The genital character and the neurotic character. In *The Psychoanalytic Reader, 1,* 148–169.

Reich, W. (1949). *Character Analysis.* New York: Orgone Institute Press.

Rosenbaum, D. P., and J. E. Beebe (1975). *Psychiatric Treatment: Crisis, Clinic, Consultation.* New York: McGraw-Hill.

Schecter, D. E. (1976). The impact of early object-relations on adult living. Lecture presented at the W. A. White Institute of Psychiatry, Psychoanalysis, and Psychology, New York, October.

Shafer, R. (1959). Generative empathy in the treatment situation. *Psychoanal. Q.* 28: 342–373.

Singer, E. (1970). *Key Concepts in Psychotherapy.* New York: Basic Books.

Small, L. (1972). Crisis therapy: Theory and method. In Goldman, G. D., and D. S. Milman (eds.), *Innovations in Psychotherapy.* Springfield, Ill.: Charles C Thomas.

Spiegel, R. (1972). Management of crises in psychotherapy. In Goldman, G. D., and G. Stricker (eds.), *Practical Problems of a Private Psychotherapy Practice.* Springfield, Ill.: Charles C Thomas.

Spotnitz, H. (1976). *Psychotherapy of Preoedipal Conditions: Schizophrenia and Severe Character Disorders.* New York: Jason Aronson.

Sullivan, H. S. (1953). *The Interpersonal Theory of Psychiatry.* New York: Norton.

_____ (1954). *The Psychiatric Interview.* New York: Norton.

Tarasoff v. *Regents of University of California* (1974). 529 P. 2d 553, 118 Cal. Rptr. 129.

Tauber, E. S., and M. R. Green (1959). *Prelogical Experience.* New York: Basic Books.

Ullman, M. (1959). The adaptive significance of the dream. *J. nerv. ment. Dis.* 129: 144–149.

Whitaker, C. A., and T. P. Malone (1953). *The Roots of Psychotherapy.* New York: McGraw-Hill.

Winnicott, D. W. (1949). Hate in the countertransference. *Int. J. Psycho-Analysis* 30: 69–74.

_____ (1965). *The Maturational Process and the Facilitating Environment.* New York: International Universities Press.

Wolberg, L. (1954). *The Technique of Psychotherapy.* New York: Grune and Stratton.

Index

73227